CREATING
INDOOR
GARDENS

CREATING
INDOOR
GARDENS

ANNE de VERTEUIL & VAL BURTON

EBURY PRESS
LONDON

Published by Ebury Press
Division of The National Magazine Company Ltd
Colquhoun House
27-37 Broadwick Street
London W1V 1FR

First impression 1986
Text © 1986 Val Burton & Anne de Verteuil
© 1986 The Paul Press Limited

ISBN 0 85223 547 X

Typeset by Peter MacDonald, Twickenham
Origination by PBD Ltd
Printed and bound in Italy by Motta, Milan

This book was edited, designed and produced by
The Paul Press Ltd, 22 Bruton Street, London W1X 7DA

Art Editor	Antony Johnson
Project Editor	Sally MacEachern
Editorial	Suzy Powling
Art Assistants	David Ayres
	Sarah McDonald
Illustrations	Gill Tomlinson
	of Jillian Burgess artists
Picture research	Liz Eddison
Index	Margaret Cooter
Art Director	Stephen McCurdy
Editorial Director	Jeremy Harwood
Publishing Director	Nigel Perryman

CONTENTS

INTRODUCTION

Designing with plants is not a new idea, but we tend to associate it with gardens rather than with indoor planting. Mainly this is because the practice of growing plants in an artificial environment is still comparatively new and innovatory. Over the last two decades our approach to architecture and design has changed dramatically, and the range of new and exciting plants continues to increase all the time. CREATING INDOOR GARDENS looks at some of the many ways in which house plants can be used with flair and imagination to suit a particular environment and to bring the garden indoors. We hope to show that form and colour can be as effectively introduced with plants as with paint and furnishings, and that some of the most successful interior designs are those which strike a happy balance between the two. Because plants are the living and volatile elements of a design, the real art lies in combining imaginative planning with practical knowledge of each plant's particular requirements. This is the challenge, and, when you succeed, it is also the reward. For those who have never considered house plants as more than pleasant or useful items of decoration, we hope that this book will change your mind, and that it will be a useful guide, and perhaps even a source of inspiration.

Anne de Verteuil
Val Burton

PART ONE

DESIGNING WITH PLANTS

LIVING ROOMS

Most people have in their minds an image of the ideal home, which lies somewhere between the attainable and the unattainable. Although necessity may dictate that you have to settle for something other than your dreams, fortunately plants are available to everyone, and they have a unique capacity to transform even the most modest living area in a quite magical way.

Assessing your room

Creating a successful interior design around living plants is a challenge that will extend both your practical skills and your imaginative ingenuity if you are to respond to it fully. To begin with, you should look at the space available objectively and candidly, noting its limitations as well as its potential. Then allow your imagination to take over and visualize the particular effect you would like to achieve. Do not be afraid to plan boldly; group planting is usually more convincing and makes a greater impact than dotting single plants here and there. Finally, give some thought to the particular characteristics of the plants themselves, and as to how they might be used to create, or suggest, the atmosphere you want. By visualizing different plants in place, you will get an idea of how radically plants can alter the character of an area. A room, for instance, which contains a group of slender weeping figs will have an altogether different feel from the same room reorganized around a collection of expansive philodendrons.

When planning a plant design, you should consider in some detail the effect that you want to create – just as you would if you were decorating with paint and paper. Are the plants to act as a foil to the decor, enhancing and complementing it, but remaining essentially in the background, or do you imagine planting which dominates and becomes a focal point in itself? Whichever is the case, your starting point must be the room itself. Its shape and size, along with its aspect and outlook are physical factors you cannot alter, but plants are a great transformer and, skilfully used, they can soften, screen, distract or emphasize.

Try thinking of the room as a garden, in terms of its scale and proportions, and consider where height is needed and where a focal point could be introduced, or an arching shape used to frame a view or an interesting corner. A well-proportioned rectangular room may need little more than plants to echo its symmetry and maintain a balance, whereas a room which is wide in proportion to its ceiling height needs a combination of upright forms emphasizing

Creating tranquillity ▷
The combination of a simple decor and a dramatic planting of ferns, palms, Ficus benjamina, Schefflera *and* Fatsia japonica *transforms this modern room into a haven of tranquillity.*

Height and light ▽
The unusual height of this dining area is enhanced not only by tall slender plants with arching forms, but also by hanging baskets.

the vertical, and broader shapes spreading into the centre. Hanging plants and cascading forms will draw the eye away from the height in a high-ceilinged room, while plants with long, tapering leaves that arch outwards will help to give the illusion of width in a narrow area, without encroaching on valuable space.

There are instances, too, where understated planting may be the most effective solution. Rooms with good period details, delicate mouldings, or other ornate features, for instance, tend to look best with discreet planting and simple, unfussy shapes. A bland or featureless room, on the other hand, can be brought to life by a display of plants with strong leaf shapes and distinctive forms.

The importance of light
The strength and distribution of light in a room will be a major factor in determining which plants can be grown and where. Except in rooms with glazed skylights, most indoor plants receive only limited amounts of light from the side. For this reason, the most successful house plants tend to be those which naturally grow in shade or filtered sunlight. As a general rule, plants with dark foliage are adapted to growing

in low light levels, often under the canopy of larger trees in tropical forests. Over-exposure to bright light will scorch and damage the leaves. Plants with brightly coloured foliage grow in the open, and need good light to maintain their colouring.

Rooms with average light conditions will suit a wide variety of plants, provided you bear their light requirements in mind when choosing their positions. However, in rooms where light is restricted, avoid dense shapes and heavy, flat greens, and use instead the acid and lime greens of shade-tolerant plants, such as *Asplenium nidus* and *Asparagus sprengeri*, as well as those with striped or interestingly patterned leaves. Begonias, with their marvellously marked and patterned leaves in shades of purple, red, brown, green and silver, cannot be bettered as foliage plants for shady rooms. Less extravagant, but no less beautiful, are the charming and rather reticent marantas, with their warm brown tones and striated leaves. *Chlorophytum* may not be particularly unusual, but it remains one of the most useful and adaptable plants for difficult and shady locations, where its unpretentious brightness will continue to shine after some of the more spectacular plants have given up the struggle.

Setting the scene

Every plant has a quality of its own, which is suggested by its form or its foliage; just like people, there are extroverted and introverted plants, the former holding centre stage while the latter remain modestly in the background. A group of rather dominating plants are the giant-leaved philodendrons, with broad spreading shapes that demand plenty of space. Like them, the well-known Swiss cheese plant, *Monstera deliciosa*, the waxy rubber plant, *Ficus elastica*, and the handsome fiddle leaf fig,.*Ficus lyrata*, are dense, sturdy plants, which will make a strong impact on a room, whether standing alone or grouped together. The effect of their imposing forms is to draw the space in, and so they are natural choices for large, open rooms. However, their talents should not be overlooked for smaller spaces where decor is plain and the strong leaf shape will be thrown into relief. *Monstera* and the mature *Philodendron bipinnatifidum*, in particular,

Plants in action △
While the strictly geometric painting to the right beckons, it is the varied planting scheme – Abutilon striatum, Dracaena marginata, Cissus *and* Pelargonium crispum – *that brings the composition to life. Containers and statuary fill out the picture.*

with their slashed and incised leaves, need to be seen without too much competition from pattern and small details. By contrast, lighter-leaved plants appear to recede into the distance, and will open up a space to give a light and airy quality. The house lime, *Sparmannia africana* and mottled *Abutilon striatum* 'Thompsonii' both have a spreading form and large soft leaves that appear almost translucent. The particular value of these plants, and others like them, is their association with light – they will make a feature at a window without blocking light or obscuring a pleasant view.

With imaginative use of decoration and lighting you can draw on the qualities of individual plants to invoke a variety of different moods. The slender grassy stems of unassuming *Cyperus* produce a cool and restful atmosphere in a room, which is markedly different from the dramatic effect of the flamboyant zebra plant, *Aphelandra squarrosa* 'Louisae'. Ferns suggest lushness and shade, while the brightly coloured *Coleus blumei* hybrids create a feeling of warmth and light.

The particular shape, or character, of a plant can be used to produce still more specific effects. *Rhoicissus rhomboidea* has dark luxuriant foliage and is equally useful as a focus, or as a screen. It can be grown as a climber and trained to frame an arch or a window, or else allowed to trail in a position where it will detract from the awkward proportions of a tall, narrow room.

By association and form, the palms and *Aspidistra* look well in formal designs – slow-growing and long-lived plants, they add a stately elegance and an air of permanence which is both pleasing and reassuring. *Yucca* and *Dracaena* have a sparse, tufty appearance, which makes them appear almost unplant-like, and which may be the reason they are so often designated as plants for modern rooms. Certainly they look superb in austerely-furnished and "high-tech" settings, but they can also introduce an unexpected, even startling, focus to a more conventional design.

Plants with fronds that are soft and feathery, such as the asparagus ferns and most of the true ferns, group well together and give a delightfully hazy effect. Their forms are "fluid" in the sense that they will merge with other, similar forms to make a soft, green mass that can be used to highlight the more arresting shape of the epiphytic stag's horn fern, *Platycerium bifurcatum*, or the clearly incised outline of the dark, glossy *Cyrtomium falcatum*.

The possibilities of associative planting are virtually endless, whether using groups of a similar habit together to obtain a harmonious effect, or introducing a sharper note with lively contrasts of outline, foliage, shape and colour. Individualists,

like the hard-edged *Sansevieria trifasciata*, look best severely alone.

Combining colours and textures

Large-leaved plants with glossy foliage look most effective against stark whites and strong colours. A room painted a rich red or vivid, dark blue offers a good setting for uncompromising plants, such as *Monstera*, *Fatsia* and *Philodendron*. If the walls are textured, marbled or mottled, with a matt finish, the sheen of the leaves adds a

A living curtain ▷

A veil of trailing foliage from a rampant passion-flower forms a delicate curtain between the inner room and the paved area beyond, which is devoted to plants, including palms and citrus fruits. The contrast of textures is contained by the repeated shape of the arch and outer door.

pleasing brilliance. Where there is plenty of good, natural light, shiny foliage against a gloss background and highly-polished surfaces can be rather hard on the eye. But in a shady, or basement room, dark walls, mirrors and a group of sleek and healthy glossy-leaved plants can make a very dramatic design, supplementing natural with reflective light.

In brightly patterned rooms, plants can be used to add a note of tranquillity. *Ficus benjamina, Cyperus, Cissus antarctica, Spathiphyllum* and all the fern family share a simplicity of effect which makes them very useful as neutralizers in a colourful scheme. This characteristic also enables them to look equally at home in a plainer setting. Striking results can be achieved by introducing colourful foliage and flowering plants as catalysts into rooms painted in the colder colours. Bromeliads, in particular, with their vivid flowering bracts and interesting leaf formations, will add an unusual and exotic flourish. A background of lush green foliage will act as a framework for the colour and provide a centre of visual interest when the flowers have died back.

Growing tropical plants
In warm and sunny rooms, a large recessed window can be adapted to house tropical

Making an impact △
It is not always necessary to use an abundance of plants to make an impact. A single, but dramatically large, palm, reflected in an impressive mirror and set off by smooth shining surfaces on all sides, makes a strong statement. Plants used in this way must be in peak condition and well cared for.

plants, such as *Dieffenbachia picta, Caladium, Codiaeum, Dizygotheca* and *Coleus* (See pp 60-63). These colourful plants need both warm temperatures and high levels of humidity – a combination which is not particularly easy to achieve in normal house conditions. One of the greatest menaces to house plants is dry air, whether from central heating or air conditioning. Plants growing in artificial conditions of dry heat require not only more frequent watering, but extra moisture in the surrounding atmosphere. Methods of caring for plants in these conditions are dealt with fully in later chapters, but you will find that by grouping plants closely together, or by growing them in the same container, they are able collectively to produce and benefit from increased humidity (*see pp 42-5*).

OPEN-PLAN LIVING

Making open-plan living interesting and visually satisfying depends to a large extent on the skill with which different areas can be created within a single space. Whatever the size and shape of your room, this is an opportunity to use plants to the full, not just for their decorative value, but also as a way of defining and screening areas where anything more solid would create physical, or visual, barriers, so blocking off valuable natural light.

The shape and dimensions of your room will necessarily determine how ambitious you can be; clearly, a large area allows greater scope for imaginative design than a small, narrow space will. Start by drawing a scale plan of the room. Block in windows, permanent features, essential storage areas and furniture. Next, mark any free areas where planting could be used effectively — either to conceal or to emphasize.

Plant planning

Areas used for cooking or eating are probably best kept relatively free of plants; for both practical reasons and for safety's

Creating warmth ▽

Long, narrow rooms create design problems that the right choice of plants can help to solve. The warm, friendly atmosphere here results from the positioning of dense-leaved Philodendron bipinnatifidum *and* Ficus elastica *to frame individual areas, without blocking light or creating unwanted obstructions. Their glossy foliage makes an attractive contrast with the rich colours and natural materials of the furnishings. All the plants chosen grow well in relatively low-light conditions.*

Group planting for a cool room ▷
The combination of cream walls, a tiled floor and strong light would be stark and over-bright without the soothing foliage of the plants, which not only creates an effective colour contrast, but also forms a screen. The bold shape of the philodendrons and the softer outline of the feathery ferns is a particularly attractive combination.

sake. The essential furniture for these areas, such as kitchen units and tables, is usually fairly obtrusive and is best counterbalanced by plants with a strong vertical form, such as dracaena, or those with a light, graceful shape, such·as *Ficus benjamina*.

Ideally, areas for sleeping and sitting should be given some privacy. By bringing the level of planting down to seating levels and by choosing plants with squat, broad shapes, you can enclose a space visually, without having to build a solid partition. *Dieffenbachia, Cordyline terminalis, Schefflera actinophylla, Yucca, Ficus elastica, Fatsia japonica, Chamaedorea elegans, Aspidistra elatior* and *Abutilon striatum* are all suitable for growing in groups on low shelving at one, or more, sides of a seating area. Your choice will depend on the amount of light available and on whether you are aiming for simplicity or for a varied effect.

Where the dimensions of a room are sufficiently large to allow a more positive definition between one area and another, place a long, rectangular container between the two areas and fill it with pots of

Philodendron selloum or climbing *P. hastatum, Fatsia, Ficus lyrata* and *Monstera deliciosa*. These plants all have dense leaves, which grow from soil level upwards, creating a decorative and highly effective screen. If you feel that a planter would introduce too firm a dividing line, use irregularly arranged, attractive wicker containers instead.

You can construct a less bulky room divider from panels of lightweight wooden trellis. Attach a strong baton along one, or more, sides of the trellis, and fix it to a wall, or to the floor. Used as a support for vigorous climbing plants, such as *Philodendron scandens* or *Rhoicissus rhomboidea*, trelliswork is ideal for concealing a bath or basin from view. *Jasminum polyanthum* forms a particularly attractive screen, as it allows light to filter through its leaves, so creating an impression of brightness and space. Although it will not flower if allowed to ramble, its charming, pointed leaves and curling tendrils will more than compensate for the lack of flowers.

Transforming a plain room △
Bold groups of Dracaena, Ficus *and* Rhoicissus
bring this rather dull, low-ceilinged room to life.
The trailing Scindapsus aureus *unifies the planting*
scheme, as well as providing interest above eye-level.
Lamps positioned on low tables help to create warmth
and intimacy.

Making the most of problem rooms

It is more difficult to delineate areas if your room is an awkward shape, but the challenge is well worth accepting. Rooms, which are square or widely-rectangular in shape, are always the most flexible, since the central floor space can be fully utilized. In narrow rooms, the inevitable passage-like effect is likely to be further emphasized by furniture and storage units, which have to be arranged to follow the lines of the walls. In such cases, deliberately planned planting should be used to create a visual interruption, thus preventing the eye from being drawn inexorably along a straight line towards the end of the room. Large blocks of plants placed at irregular intervals on either side of the room will create hidden areas and provide visual interest. Where space allows, the arrangements can be bold — designed to attract immediate attention. Use plants with sturdy architectural shapes, such as *Monstera*, *Ficus* and any of the philodendrons. In areas with limited space, the arching, less obtrusive shapes of *Ficus benjamina* and *Dracaena* will produce a similar visual effect, but without causing a physical obstruction.

It is not uncommon for a long, narrow room to be a conversion from two smaller rooms. This often gives the uneasy effect of a room that falls into two distinct halves. If the room is very narrow, the most effective solution may be to emphasize the division by growing plants around the 'arch' on wires, or on strips of trelliswork, so that the two spaces are framed with greenery. If space allows, flat-backed pots can be attached to the wall on either side of the arch and filled with trailing plants.

High-ceilinged rooms

Living in a small room requires inventive use of space. High-ceilinged rooms provide extra areas for shelves and cupboards but, on the other hand, these added structures may make the room unbalanced or oppressive. Hanging planters have a softening effect, as well as the added benefit of not taking up any floor space.

If hanging containers are impractical, fix a shelf above head height along a sunny wall and use it for trailing and arching plants. The shelf should be wide enough to accommodate the plants' spread and also be easily accessible for regular watering as hanging plants on high shelves will dry out more quickly than ground-level plants.

A large-scale arrangement of plants will always look more effective if the plants are grouped at different levels. Plants on a high shelf should be balanced by plants positioned closer to the floor. Similarly, plants arranged on shelves look best when placed in random groups at different levels so that your design consists of splashes of greenery and colour both above and below eye level.

Planting for effect ▽
The shiny, dark foliage of this exuberant Rhoicissus *forms a striking contrast with the white walls, but does not distract attention from the collection of sculpture and china.*

**Plants in
awkward corners** ◁
*Plants cascading downwards
soften the strong vertical lines
of this high-ceilinged room. The*
Hedera canariensis *will climb
upwards, framing the passage
with greenery — an imaginative
way of using plants to brighten
an otherwise uninteresting area.*

Light
Your choice and arrangement of plants
obviously depends to a large extent on the
position of windows and the distribution of
light. In large, open-plan rooms the scope
for extensive and exciting planting is
enormous; whereas cold, sunless rooms are
more difficult, as the less light a plant
receives, the less vigorous its growth will
be. One solution is to use mirrors to deflect
light into dark corners; another is to choose
shade-tolerant plants, such as *Aglaonema,
Aspidistra* and ferns.

If the room is very dark, it is better to
concentrate on one particularly effective
arrangement close to a window. A recessed
window is the perfect spot for such a
feature; however, flat windows can be
transformed by fixing wooden, or glass,

shelves across them. Mirrored shelves can
produce a sensational effect, throwing back
fragmented reflections of the plants and
catching all the available light.

Making the most of architectural features
If your room has attractive features, such as
wide windowsills, a mantlepiece, niches or
alcoves, plants can be used to draw
attention to them, as well as being
decorative in their own right. If you are
fortunate enough to have a room with a
glazed skylight, it will provide near-perfect
light conditions for plants; whether hanging
or standing beneath it.

Pillars and columns can be enhanced by
growing plants up them. If the pillars are
unattractive, cover them with mesh (nylon
or fine wire), which will provide support for

climbers, such as *Philodendron scandens*, *Rhoicissus rhomboidea* or large-leaved *Tetrastigma voinierianum*. Plants grown in this way must be carefully maintained and frequently checked for dead and browning foliage.

Fireplaces are frequently cited and illustrated as being ideal places for growing plants, but this is really only practical if the chimney has been sealed, protecting plants from down-draughts and dust, and if the plants receive adequate light. Plants with a brief flowering period are probably the best choice, but, on the whole, it is better to avoid the temptation.

When using plants to decorate your room, remember that the most successful schemes are not necessarily the most lavish; a simple idea, if it is imaginative or unexpected, can transform an otherwise uninteresting space.

Forming screens ▽
Densely-leaved plants in attractive baskets make a very effective screen, which divides this large room into separate areas without detracting from its spacious atmosphere. Varying heights and variegated foliage will add extra interest to any such plant group.

21

HALLS & STAIRWAYS

Halls, staircases and landings are transitional areas within the home, and consequently tend not to be places where people linger for long. They are, however, continually on display, even if only briefly, so there is every reason to make them as pleasant as possible, both for yourself and for your visitors. Halls are particularly important in this respect, since they give visitors their initial impression of your home, so why not make them immediately welcoming through the addition of a few, well-chosen foliage or bright, flowering plants? But, whatever you plan, remember that conditions in the average hall are often far from ideal for the majority of house plants; therefore it is important to make a realistic assessment of the area before placing any plants.

Brightening your hall
The most obvious limitation is likely to be lack of light, since, unless there is a window or the hall is part of an open-plan area, it will often be quite dark (in some cases, daylight may even be non-existent). Other important factors to consider are the actual shape and size of the space, and the temperature.

If there is a window, a cool hall is an ideal location for many annual or perennial flowering house plants, provided they are standing in, or close to, the light. With a little forethought you can plan a succession of plants to flower from winter through to spring, creating a point of interest that changes with the seasons.

In winter, flowering bulbs bring a welcome reminder of spring – narcissi, tulips and crocuses will thrive in cool temperatures: A bowl of hyacinths placed near the door provides the added bonus of delicious fragrance, as will *Jasminum polyanthum*. Remember to cut back the jasmine after flowering as this is essential if it is to flower the following year.

Cyclamen persicum, *Azalea* and the Christmas cactus, *Schlumbergera* × 'Buckleyi', will add bright splashes of colour, but need good light to perform really well. When these have finished flowering, you can replace them with *Cineraria*, *Senecio cruentus*, *Lilium longiflorum* and flamboyant *Calceolaria*, followed by summer-flowering *Schizanthus*, *Celosia* and *Exacum affine*.

You can try something unconventional, too. It is not often realized, for instance, that hydrangeas will grow indoors. Their long-lasting flowers and tolerance of quite low light levels make them excellent temporary plants for halls, where they provide a touch of splendour as well as creating a bridge between the indoor and the outdoor garden. The flowers of *Hydrangea* should not be removed, but it is important to deadhead all other flowering plants regularly. This is not purely for aesthetic reasons, but also to prolong the flowering period.

It is tempting to soften the strong vertical lines of a hall by growing large spreading plants there, but unless the area is larger than average they will only cause an obstruction, and suffer damage as a result. Instead, choose the upright form of plants like *Dracaena*, which will create a strong impact, particularly in an uncluttered setting.

The art of display
Decorative containers of any kind make good features in their own right. It is worth spending some time and thought over their selection, especially for a hall, where everything is very much on view, and your

Adding warmth ▷
Dense planting on a purpose-built platform rescues an open staircase from austerity. Large-leaved Sparmannia *revel in the light and add height to the group, while still allowing light to filter through the leaves. Philodendrons, ferns, Ficus and Rhoicissus grow happily in the semi-shade.*

choice of plants may be limited. The right container will highlight a decorative scheme, and should emphasize a plant, without overpowering it. Tall plants do not always need large pots, but tend to look unbalanced, which indeed they often are, unless placed in a larger outer container.

A plant pedestal makes an excellent display stand where space is limited, for the arching form of the Boston fern, *Nephrolepis exaltata* 'Bostoniensis', or for the more formal lines of an *Aspidistra*. The pedestal can be turned easily, so that plants growing in shaded spots are encouraged to develop a full and even shape.

Another good way of displaying plants in a confined area is to use raised planting troughs that will fit against the wall and take up the minimum width. Choose plants of varying shapes and heights so as to avoid a regimented look.

Where there is room for a table large enough to accommodate a display plant, the Norfolk Island pine, *Araucaria*, or a small *Monstera deliciosa* make imposing choices in a dark area. In a lighter spot, *Cyperus alternifolius* is a graceful feature.

Staircases and landings
Happily, staircases and landings are generally far easier areas to plant successfully. If there is not enough light in the hall to make planting viable, it is better to concentrate on using positions on, or near, a landing window instead, so as to draw the eye on and upwards.

If the house has an open stairwell, you can exploit its height and the extra sense of space it provides to the full by using hanging plants and cascading foliage.

Inevitably light will dictate which plants will be most suitable. Where there is both good light and warmth, the beautiful bromeliads will make a brilliant hanging feature or, in very warm, humid conditions, the glorious scarlet flowering trailer, *Columnea microphylla*. If temperatures are not high enough to support dramatic flowering plants such as these, you can use form to make an impact of a different kind. *Platycerium bifurcatum*, for example, has a strong sculptural shape that looks most striking when framed in a window on a simple, modern stairway.

Enclosed staircases and landings can be brightened with hanging baskets filled with ivies, *Tradescantia*, *Davallia canariensis*, or the asparagus ferns. *Ceropegia woodii* with its diminutive, heart-shaped leaves is a charming feature for a tiny staircase window. *Jasminum polyanthum*, or *Ficus pumila*, grown in a hanging container, can be encouraged to grow across a fanlight to make a delightful tracery effect.

Making use of wasted space ◁
A group of Phoenix palms placed at the foot of a stairwell rise gracefully to the top, where light from above emhasizes the strong lines of their arching fronds. In this otherwise lost space the palms thrive and prosper. Their green and curving shapes, while impressive in themselves, serve to soften the vertical lines of the balustrade. In this deceptively simple partnership each element complements the other, and the minimal use of colour heightens the effect.

Softening a modern staircase ▷
The severe lines of this staircase in a modern, open-plan house provide the perfect setting for a profusion of plants that curve, climb or trail. Philodendron scandens spills over the edges, while Rhoicissus rhomboidea (top left) makes a dense leaf cover in contrast to the fragile outline of Dizygotheca at its side. All benefit from good overhead light filtered by blinds.

By using the same variety of plant in the hall and on a stair window, you can link the two areas visually, giving a pleasing continuity of effect. Plants can be changed around between the two from time to time, which will benefit those which may be growing in less favourable conditions. On a staircase, climbing plants can really come into their own. Two plants that will grow with great rapidity are the chestnut vine, *Tetrastigma voinierianum* and the sweetheart plant, *Philodendron scandens*.

Artificial light
A spotlight on the ceiling above the corner of a staircase should provide sufficient light to stimulate the growth of shade-tolerant plants, such as *Rhoicissus rhomboidea*. But, where the overall level of light is very poor, it may be worth installing an artificial light planter to enable you to grow some of the more unusual and brightly coloured varieties. Growing plants under artificial light is described on p 141.

KITCHENS

The kitchen is often the focal point of the household — a place where people gather to cook, eat and talk — so it is not surprising that it is also a popular spot for growing indoor plants. At the same time, its practical purpose makes it a room with particular environmental idiosyncrasies, which could constitute a real hazard to some plants; these include fluctuating temperatures, blasts of hot, dry air, steam, smoke, gas fumes, and draughts. Your planting needs to be carefully planned to take these factors into consideration.

Choosing the plants
When choosing plants, it is important to remember that the temperature may change quite dramatically during the course of an average working day, particularly in winter. For changeable conditions like these, it is safest to select a core of reliable plants, such as *Chlorophytum*, *Tradescantia*, the asparagus ferns, *Chamaedorea elegans*, and some of the tougher ferns — *Davallia canariensis*, *Platycerium bifurcatum*, and *Asplenium bulbiferum*. All tolerate cooler conditions, but also appreciate humidity.

Plants for a family kitchen ◁
Welcoming and warm, and bursting with decorative detail, this family kitchen is animated by plants which link up to the conservatory beyond. Tall standing palms are wisely situated out of the main thoroughfare, while a trailing Scindapsus aureus introduces a splash of compatible colour in the corner.

Cutting down the clutter ◁
The plants in this dazzlingly streamlined kitchen have been cleverly situated to soften its somewhat clinical appearance without disturbing its efficiency. Suspended above head height, pots of Philodendron scandens *frame the view of the garden. On the left,* Dracaena fragrans *and* Yucca *display their simple shapes to advantage.*

areas are not suitable for planting.

In small, or galley, kitchens, standing specimen plants are rarely practical, because there are few, if any, areas where they will not be in the way. For the same reason, frequently-used work surfaces are best kept free, since no plant will thrive if being constantly moved, while there is also the possibility that foliage will become dusted with fine substances such as flour, which can block leaf pores and interfere with transpiration. Instead, concentrate on planting in positions away from the main areas of activity. A piece of pegboard, painted and attached to the wall, makes an attractive and space-saving feature when covered with climbing and trailing plants, fixed in pot-holders at different levels.

Hanging baskets and containers are ideal if kept just above head height, either in the centre of the room, or around a window. Easy access to plants is important, so you should avoid placing them on high shelves, or on the tops of cupboards, where light is poor and space cramped.

Matching plants to decor
Where there is sufficient light, shelving is the obvious place to display small and medium-sized plants. You can make full use of such planting to complement, or to contrast with, the background wall colour. A plain white kitchen can be warmed up by boldly-coloured plants such as *Aphelandra squarrosa*, climbing *Scindapsus aureus*, or the more muted shades of *Begonia rex* and *Maranta leuconeura*. Conversely, deep warm yellows will offset the fresh greens of *Asplenium nidus* and *Asparagus sprengeri* beautifully. Angles and hard lines can be masked and softened with arching shapes and fine leaf forms. Try *Asparagus plumosus*, tumbling *Pilea nummularifolia*, mossy-looking pots of green and golden *Helxine*, or the soft-leaved *Tolmeia*.

Pale stripped-wood surfaces and dark green foliage make a pleasing contrast.

In a family home with small children, on the other hand, the kitchen could be in use for most of the day, so you can increase the range of plants to include those which need even levels of warmth and humidity. *Asplenium nidus, Pilea cadierei, Peperomia caperata,* and the attractively variegated *Codiaeum* are all suitable.

Most plants are better kept away from gas fumes, which can present problems in a small space. However, *Aspidistra elatior* and *Rhoicissus rhomboidea,* in particular, seem relatively immune, provided they receive some ventilation.

Positioning the plants
In new apartment blocks and buildings, the kitchen is often designed to make the most economical use of space, so opportunities for planting may be limited. This can be particularly frustrating if the room receives a large amount of light, but it is best to be realistic at the outset, and to decide which

A single, healthy specimen of *Aspidistra*, in particular, is hard to beat. Somewhat similar in foliage effect, *Spathiphyllum* is well worth the extra attention it requires, as it is a beautiful plant for a warm kitchen where it will bloom through the summer. Remember, though, that both these plants need space and should not be crammed in where they cannot grow comfortably, both upwards and outwards. In tighter spaces, try *Rhoicissus rhomboidea*, unsupported, so that it will cascade downwards.

A period dresser gives a comfortable and informal air to a kitchen, which can be accentuated by using old-fashioned plants such as *Asparagus plumosus*, or the charming small *Pteris* ferns that seem to be naturally associated with country living. However, these ferns need a high level of humidity to prevent the delicate fronds from drying and curling. They will look their best and also grow well, if planted together in groups and kept in an outer container of moist peat, or sphagnum moss.

Kitchen style
Kitchens which are also family rooms tend to accumulate a variety of odds and ends. While other people's clutter always looks more interesting than one's own, there is no doubt that this type of crowded room can be enormously attractive. Plants in this kind of setting are best kept together in groups, not only for effect, but to prevent them from being overlooked. Where the more unobtrusive foliage plants are liable to go unnoticed, use flowering plants, such as *Impatiens* with its simple, clear-coloured flowers, to make a bright splash on a windowsill, or on a table near a window.

If you have a streamlined kitchen, where most of your equipment is stored in cupboards and decoration is minimal, you can use plants to add a touch of drama: the spiky outline of *Dracaena*, the bold shape of a large, thornless cactus, or the classic lines of the smaller palms will stand out against an uncluttered background. On the other hand, tiny plants, whose appeal lies in the detail of their shape and foliage, may be overwhelmed by such a setting, but look at home on crowded shelves. *Hypoestes sanguinolenta*, *Pellaea rotundifolia*, *Senecio rowleyanus* and *Ceropegia woodii* are all small

plants, quite distinct from each other, but sharing a curious charm, even quirkiness, which can be used to great effect to highlight a collection of personal treasures.

Herbs
Herbs, of course, are the most obvious choice of plant for the kitchen. Chives, parsley, basil and many other herbs can be grown in pots on a sunny windowsill, or as a feature, in the form of a small hanging garden. Each herb is best grown in a separate pot to suit individual watering requirements, and either kept in hanging baskets, or placed together in a lightweight plastic container suspended on wires. If growing the herbs together, ensure that excess water is not allowed to stand in the outer container after watering. Parsley looks fresh and decorative grown in a round clay container perforated like a strawberry pot.

Window display
Take full advantage of a windowsill above a sink for growing plants which enjoy an occasional steam bath: saintpaulias, ferns, marantas, *Peperomia caperata*, *Pilea cadierei* and *P. nummularifolia* will grow well in a warm window, shaded from direct sunlight. It is essential to give these plants adequate protection from draughts and from cold night temperatures, in the form of a well-fitting blind, or curtains. If this is impossible, at least move them to a warmer spot in winter.

In a cool kitchen, a beautiful summer flowering arrangement can be made on a well-lit, but sunless sill, with pale blue *Plumbago capensis*, pink *Fuchsia* and pots of dark green, or variegated, ivy. The ivy can be trained to frame the whole window, or allowed to trail down from suitably placed hanging pots.

In a quite different mood, an undemanding choice for a small, sunny window might be a collection of succulents. Arranged on shelves across the window in an assortment of shapes and sizes. They will make a fascinating, and slightly bizarre, array silhouetted against the light. Cacti naturally grow in extremes of searing daytime heat and freezing night-time cold, so they can do without protection. Succulents, however, prefer less extreme conditions (*see pp 54-9*).

Brightening a dull corner △
*With no window to provide a distracting view, this
utilitarian corner deserves the touch of refreshing
colour given it by this plant grouping. Light from
above, humidity from steamy water and adequate
space offer the perfect situation for variegated
dracaenas (far right),* Asplenium nidus *(in
foreground) and* Tolmeia.

BATHROOMS

Bathrooms present all indoor gardeners with something of a challenge. How best can you deal with a room offering enormous visual potential for planting, but where conditions are often far from ideal for plants? Fluctuating temperatures, irregular bursts of humidity, and, frequently, poor lighting, are some of the hazards that plants have to contend with in the average bathroom. But there are plants that will withstand these conditions, and by careful selection and planning, you will be able to create a healthy and attractive planting scheme to enliven any bathroom.

Assessing your bathroom
Points that you will need to consider are the size of the room, its decorative style and

Brightening up bathrooms △
Limited space has been maximized by using a made-to-measure planting container. Filled with a variety of plants its concentration of greenery becomes the focal point of the room, contrasting in texture and colour with the pristine white surfaces.

colour scheme, the amount and intensity of light it receives, and the temperature levels. All these factors are inter-related; the particular difficulty of plant planning for a bathroom is the balancing of one against another and deciding when and where to make a compromise.

If you are redesigning your bathroom, this is the ideal time to organize shelf space — recessed shelves, backed by mirrors with concealed lighting, provide wonderful display areas for exotically-coloured plants.

30

**A garden in
your bathroom** ◁
*When there is plenty of light
and space, there too is the
opportunity for confident
planting schemes. Here* Fatsia
japonica, *philodendrons,*
Schefflera, *begonias and*
Ficus elastica *combine with
ferns to create a bathroom in
which the plants themselves,
thriving in ideal conditions, are
the dominant and completely
appropriate decorative element.*

Widened bath surrounds are ideal for groups
of larger plants grown close together.

As always, light is the key to the kind of
plants that can be grown, so, even if you
are not planning any major alterations,
it is well worth considering how you can
maximize the amount of light in the room.
A simple solution is to use an all-white
theme. This will brighten a shaded
bathroom and have the added advantage of
making the foliage stand out clearly. If your
preference is for muted colours and the
light level is low, then it is best to
concentrate plants in the window area. A
group of plants arranged on a shelf across a
window makes an attractive focal point. If
possible extend the shelf into the corner to
make a useful space for jars and bottles.

In small bathrooms, keep the design
simple. Too many details make the space
appear smaller. Well-placed mirrors work
wonders in the smallest space, especially if
placed opposite a window, when they will
increase the lighting level dramatically.
Plants placed so that their reflection is
captured by a mirror on the opposite wall
will distract the eye from hard angles and
corners, and increase the sense of space still
further. Even one plant will cheat the eye,
if not the mind, into believing there are
many more.

Choosing the plants
Choose plants to fit the scale of the room.
A large feature plant will look sensational
in a large bathroom where there is enough

space to allow some variation in temperature and humidity levels. On the other hand, a large plant in a small bathroom is apt to look overpowering and also to deteriorate in such a confined space. The scale of smaller-leaved plants is generally more suitable for small rooms, particularly if conditions are likely to cause periodic leaf fall. The loss of a few leaves will be far less noticeable on, say, a *Ficus pumila*, or an asparagus fern, than on a large-leaved philodendron, where one lost leaf will ruin the whole effect.

There are several advantages to growing plants in groups. You make maximum use of space, while ensuring that each plant benefits from the micro-climate created by the transpiration of the others. Variety of shading, shape, and leaf variegation creates an attractive display, full of detail and interest, and any plant which fails can be easily removed without spoiling the total effect.

Choose plants which are in keeping with the style of the room. The spear-like, upright leaves of *Sansevieria trifasciata* will emphasize vertical lines and introduce a note of formality, while the graceful arching form of the parlour palm, *Chamaedorea elegans*, makes a splendid plant for a "period" bathroom.

In a large bathroom, a bromeliad tree will make a truly dramatic impact. The myriad shades, colours and variegations of this fascinating family of plants must provide a tempting proposition for the ambitious indoor gardener. One branch suspended on wire from the ceiling will allow sufficient surface area for many different specimens. Choose colours that complement the decor, keeping to the less flamboyant varieties if the walls are strongly patterned (*see pp 68-71*).

Strong design features are best complemented by simple planting. Where there is a fine bath or decorated hand basin, introduce plants with subdued, or plain green, foliage. In this way the impact of the feature will be heightened rather than submerged in a discordant array of pattern and colour. On the other hand, the delicate leaves of a plant like *Calathea* are seen to best advantage in a fairly neutral setting, which places the emphasis on the plant.

A touch of the exotic
In a constantly warm and steamy bathroom, make the most of the conditions to create a tropical area. These conditions quite closely reflect the natural habitat of the Araceae — philodendrons, *Monstera* and the goose foot plant, *Syngonium podophyllum* — which provide bold displays when grouped together in a large bathroom.

If you keep the temperature consistently above 18°C (65°F), you will be able to grow these, and some of the other, more brilliant foliage plants. *Maranta, Dracaena godseffiana, Fittonia* and *Peperomia* species all flourish in high temperatures, and are

A touch of luxury ◁
*Taking a bath becomes an
exercise in the exotic, with
orchids on all sides and the
beautiful dark green veining
on the translucent leaves of a
caladium displayed in full light.
The fine windows need no
adornment, drawing the eye to
yet more greenery outside.*

certainly worth considering if you have
individual thermostats on your radiators.

In cooler bathrooms, *Aspidistra*, ferns and
variegated ivies will all grow well, and,
where space allows, a hanging basket of
Saxifraga stolonifera will add extra colour.
Platycerium bifurcatum, the stag's horn fern,
is often seen at its best in a bathroom,
where it can be easily plunged into the bath
for watering.

Plant care
These difficult growing conditions mean
that every plant will need careful
maintenance, with particular attention paid
to individual watering needs. Because water
is immediately available, bathroom plants
tend to be over- rather than under-watered.
In hard water areas, it is always a good idea
to keep a jug and atomizer filled with water,
which has been allowed to stand, rather
than watering direct from the tap.

Wipe leaves frequently, particularly if
they become dusted with talcum powder,
and avoid using aerosols too close to plants,
as this can also have the effect of clogging
the pores and filtering the light supply.
Bear in mind that some plants will benefit
from the occasional move to more clement
conditions.

BEDROOMS

A bedroom is not usually the first place that springs to mind for growing plants; in fact, it is very often the final resting place for plants that have failed to thrive in every other room in the house. After all, bedrooms are seldom used except at night, so there is less incentive to decorate them with plants. In addition, bedrooms are usually cooler than the rest of the house and it is likely that visits to them will be brief, and will not include time for checking plants.

However, these apparently discouraging factors are, in themselves, rather positive ones as far as the plants are concerned. Plants here are less likely to be moved around or to suffer from stuffy or smoky atmospheres. It is true that they are also unlikely to be given as much attention,

but, if conditions are cool, this is not necessarily a drawback — overwatering can kill just as surely as underwatering. Any failures are likely to be the result of the wrong choice of plant for the conditions, or simply because the plant has already been moved too often and so has tried to adapt to too many changes of light and temperature before arriving in the bedroom.

Lower temperatures suit a surprising number of tropical, as well as temperate,

Providing contrast ▽
In the airy lightness of this spacious bedroom a fine specimen of Ficus benjamina *grows well, its form a pleasing contrast to the mound of helxine on the table. These two suffice to provide light relief from the strong vertical lines of the bedstead, the lamp and the impressive tiled stove.*

plants, because of the greater degree of moisture retained in the atmosphere. Many ferns, for instance, brown and drop fronds in centrally-heated rooms; two of the most popular, *Adiantum capillus-veneris* and *Nephrolepis exaltata* 'Bostoniensis' will tolerate temperatures as low as 10-13°C (50-55°F) without any ill effects.

Although plants in lower temperatures need watering less often, they must never — particularly the ferns — be allowed to dry out completely. It is well worth keeping both an atomizer and a full jug of water conveniently at hand, as a reminder.

Choosing containers for effect △
A cool and tranquil composition for a bedroom where the window gets no direct sun. The foliage of a nephrolepis fern placed at the highest point makes an attractive contrast with the glossy surfaces of Philodendron *and the exotic lipstick vine* Aeschynanthus, *trailing over the table edge.*

Choosing the plants
If a room is unheated, aspect will obviously be an influential factor. A cool, sunless room is generally a more daunting proposition than a room which is warmed by a few hours of sunlight a day. Two quite

**Plant groups for
the windowsill** ▷
*A still life in green and white,
this composition of textures
draws on plants, containers and
sculpture to concoct a totally
successful scheme. The plants
have been chosen to provide
variety not only in terms of
colour and form but also of
botanical type. Together here
are Abutilon, Ficus,
Campanula isophylla 'Alba'
(in flower), cactus, helxine,
feathery Asparagus sprengeri
and Poinsettia. A group of
plants near a radiator will need
frequent spraying; even so the
heat should be kept low.*

large and very handsome plants that will grow in cool, shady conditions are *Araucaria excelsa*, the Norfolk Island pine, and the silk oak, *Grevillea robusta*. *Aspidistra*, with its tolerant nature, makes a good alternative and takes up rather less space. *Yucca* is another suitable feature plant for cool conditions, but it needs good light to grow really well.

For rooms with cool to moderate temperatures, choose plants such as climbing *Cissus antarctica*, glossy-leaved *Cyrtomium falcatum* and *Asparagus plumosus*. *Cissus* dislikes disturbance, which makes it a good candidate for a bedroom. Hederas of all kinds like cool shade, with a degree of moisture in the air and will grow exuberantly in infrequently used rooms. Since shade-tolerant plants are mostly dark-leaved, they tend to create a cool, restful atmosphere which seems appropriate in a bedroom. However, in a dark-walled or heavily patterned room they may produce a rather sombre effect which can be lifted by growing them in brightly coloured or white containers.

Where there is good light, cool bedrooms are ideal for flowering plants. *Streptocarpus*, *Polyanthus*, *Plumbago*, *Hydrangea* and *Campanula isophylla*, in cool shades of blue and white, will complement a collection of foliage plants and flower throughout the summer. Winter-flowering *Cyclamen* and Japanese azalea, which tend to wilt dramatically in heat, will grow and flower better in cool temperatures, as will sweetly-scented *Jasminum polyanthum*. Unheated, sunny bedrooms will suit pelargoniums, both the zonal and trailing varieties; a mixture of pinks and whites adds great charm to a simple country bedroom.

Bedrooms also make suitable places for resting plants in the winter. Cacti and succulents can spend their winter resting period in the bedroom, as can plants such as *Chamaerops*, × *Fatshedera* and *Tradescantia*.

If you prefer the idea of plants that will be trouble-free and require minimal care, a collection of the curious, and almost entirely self-sufficient, airplants, *Tillandsia*, make a serene and fascinating display. Mounted on bark, driftwood or coral, their grey-green tendrils seem midway between living plant and sculpture (*see pp 68-71*).

CONSERVATORIES

Besides the pleasure of having a specific area that attracts the maximum light, a glazed room of any kind is a truly invaluable asset for the enthusiastic plant grower. As your collection of plants expands and your expertise increases, so, too, in all probability, will your dissatisfaction with the means currently at your disposal to grow them. Temperature levels are reasonably controllable but, more often than not, it is lack of light that will thwart your ambitions.

If you are fortunate enough to have a conservatory already attached to your home, then the problem is resolved, and your only decision will be the pleasant one of deciding how to realize its potential to the full. However, if you are planning to extend your home by the addition of a conservatory, or some other form of glazed extension, you can take full advantage of a warm and sunny aspect to build on a room which will accommodate both you and your plants to the mutual benefit of both.

Any room which incorporates a large area of glass into its design will immediately open up the range of plants that you can grow. However, the most effective distribution of light comes from glazed roofs pitched at an angle of some 50° in the style of a greenhouse, or true conservatory. The great advantage of growing sensitive plants under glass is that it combines near-perfect natural light conditions with protection against cold. The possible disadvantage is that in cold weather, your extensive source of light becomes an extensive area of potential heat loss, which may be further emphasized by the fact that most extensions are, by definition, exposed on at least two, and possibly more, sides.

Unheated conservatories
Conservatories and sun porches are often used as fair-weather rooms and may become very hot in summer. In rooms that receive full sun, you can use the area directly beneath the glass for hanging cacti and succulents. Many flowering plants will also thrive in these warm light conditions. But in winter, temperatures can fall, so, if the conservatory is unheated, it is advisable to grow a protective framework of hardier plants and to take the precaution of moving tender specimens into warmer rooms until temperatures rise again.

A cool conservatory, or garden room, need never be an uninteresting place. In fact, it is important that it should not be so, because even if you do not spend much time there in cold weather, it will probably be plainly visible from adjoining rooms. Any of the plants described in the Indoors/Outdoors section (*see pp 76-9*) as suitable for sheltered outdoor locations will thrive in these conditions. An evergreen background can be composed of bold foliage plants such as *Fatsia* and × *Fatshedera*, combined with the spikier outlines of the fan palm, *Chamaerops humilis* and *Yucca*. The many varieties of *Hedera helix*, both green and variegated, can be made to climb and trail in shaded corners with some of the hardy ferns.

In summer the room can be ablaze with colour from annual and deciduous climbers, as well as fuchsias, pelargoniums and trailing *Campanula isophylla*. A grape vine trained across a glass roof is both picturesque and useful, providing grapes if there is sufficient sun to ripen them, and leaves for stuffed vine leaves. A vine will also filter the light, creating a suitable environment for ferns, epiphytic bromeliads and some of the more-easily cultivated

The charm of a conservatory ▷
An oasis of colour and rampant greenery on a hot summer's day, this sunny and inviting conservatory is filled with a profusion of flowers. Trailing fuchsias and ivy-leafed pelargoniums in shades of pink and mauve tangle with delicate ferns and abundant ivies, while a grape-vine basks above.

orchids — either grown in hanging baskets, or on moss and wire structures.

A cool conservatory is also an excellent place for resting flowering desert cacti that need cold winter conditions to encourage flowering the following season. Do not water these cacti until spring, for a combination of damp and cold will prove fatal to them.

Heated conservatories

If you can provide some form of general background heating to keep temperatures up during the winter, you can grow an almost unlimited diversity of plants.
A minimum winter temperature of 10°C (50°F) will enable you to grow many foliage plants and three fragrant flowering plants, all with white flowers, *Gardenia jasminoides*, *Stephanotis floribunda* and *Hoya bella*. Allow *Stephanotis* to clamber up and *Hoya* to trail downwards.

There are some plants that seem to have a natural affinity with light, and look somewhat dull and uninteresting when positioned away from it. The house lime, *Sparmannia africana* is one such example. If given plenty of space, it will spread its large, pale, downy leaves outwards in a pleasantly untidy way, and will also produce white flowers in the early spring. Another light-lover is *Abutilon striatum*

Controlled profusion △
Growing a number of plants in a limited space can sometimes have a claustrophobic effect, but here the combination succeeds where one plant, a magnificent Hydrangea macrophylla, *dominates the scheme and where meticulous care creates an indoor garden of order and calm. Among fuchsias in the raised bed* Jasminum *clambers upwards to mingle with plumbago and geraniums tumbling from pots attached to the support posts.*

'Thompsonii', with its mottled green and yellow leaves and beautiful bell-shaped orange flowers, which appear intermittently throughout the summer. Both do well in a temperate conservatory; of the two *Sparmannia* is the hardier.

Light

The quality and intensity of light received will depend on the aspect, and it will be a matter of chance as to whether this is predominantly warm or cool. Even so, conditions within the room itself will vary from bright, direct, and sunless light to indirect and shaded light. Areas near the glazing will receive maximum sun and warmth, but will also be the most vulnerable, since they will heat up quickly during the day and lose heat rapidly in the evening and in winter. It is very important, therefore, to fit windows with roller, or slatted, blinds, that will give shade from intense heat and protection against the cold. Grade plants according to their individual light requirements, using those in the front rank to shelter those behind. If the effect you want to achieve is of massed foliage, trailing, climbing and crowding round a judiciously placed table and chairs, you may choose to arrange plants informally, using tall standing specimens to break the lines, with perhaps a narrow shelf around the perimeter for flowering plants. This will be the perfect setting for an elaborate jardinière planted with ferns and trailing plants. The Victorians, who translated the science of growing plants under glass into magnificent edifices of glass and metal, were fond of using these tiered wire, or wrought-iron, containers to decorate their conservatories and extravagantly landscaped "winter gardens".

Humidity

Slatted wooden shelving, or staging, will give a structured effect, but is undoubtedly the best way to grow a large selection of smaller plants together, since it minimizes the labour of watering and tending. Trays can be lined with capillary matting, which means that plants are able to absorb water as and when they need it. This close grouping will also be beneficial in terms of humidity — hence its particular suitability for small plants in rooms that are kept heated throughout the year.

Glazed extensions, that are also used as living rooms all year round, will benefit from solar heat in the summer, but will probably be heated in the same way as the rest of the house, so that the familiar problem of dry heat may re-assert itself. If you are taking advantage of the light to grow some of the very colourful tropical foliage and flowering plants that need both warmth and high humidity, it may be worth using a small room humidifier.

Window conservatories

Another marvellous Victorian invention is the window conservatory — a miniature greenhouse attached to the outside of a window. These structures, occasionally still to be seen in period houses, are now fast regaining popularity, not least because of the fantastic opportunities they offer to apartment-dwellers and to people in houses with limited space for plants. Window conservatories are manufactured in a variety of styles, from simple aluminium and glass structures to reproductions of Victorian models, with built-in adjustable shelving.

The range of plants that can be grown will depend on the aspect. Bright sunny windows are ideal for cacti and succulents, *Coleus*, and other sun-loving plants. Most window conservatories are fitted with a hinged, sloping roof window that can be opened for extra ventilation, and if humidity is not crucial to the plants you are growing, you may prefer to remove the internal house window altogether. On the other hand, plants that need humidity will do better in the micro-climate created by a closed environment, and in this case, you should leave the internal window in place. A drip tray fitted into the base of the conservatory can be kept filled with water to increase humidity.

Using plant stands ▽
In this small conservatory white painted wrought ironwork and a tiered metal plant stand provide architectural features of great charm as a setting for a spring collection. Pots of bulbs and Azalea indica make a welcome splash of colour.

PLANT GROUPING

When you see plants ranged together in a local garden centre or plant shop, it is easy to forget that a plant's origins will determine its suitability, and to be seduced into buying it solely for its value as a decorative object. This is a mistaken approach. Any professional will tell you that knowledge of a plant's natural environment will make it easier for you to combine plants successfully in groups. House plants come from many different regions of the world, and their habitats include the physical and climatic extremes of tropical jungle and desert terrain, as well as the more moderate conditions of the temperate zones.

When designing with non-indigenous plants in an artificial environment, success depends on two factors: reconstruction of the most suitable conditions, and a setting which shows the plants to best advantage. In most instances, these two elements of the design process are so closely linked as to be inseparable.

Plant associations

Except in adverse conditions, plants rarely grow singly, but tend to form groups.

Observation of the way in which plants grow and relate to each other in the wild will help you when you are planning an arrangement that is to include several plants in close proximity, or even in the same container.

The process by which any successful group of plants forms an association is invariably the result of the specific environment in which the plants have evolved, or, as is often the case, been introduced artificially. As a result of geographical location and local climate, certain environments are more generally favourable to plant life than others, and in these areas, highly complex hierarchies may evolve. A tropical rain forest, for example, contains many plants of different sizes and growing habits, ranging from the tallest trees supporting lianas, lichens and epiphytic plants, down to the smallest ground-hugging creeper growing in the rich leaf litter of the forest floor. Each of these plants is, in varying degrees, dependent on the others for the continued stability of its environment. It is this mutually assured security which gives rise to the rich diversity of shapes, the lush foliage, and the often extravagant flowers, which make these tropical plants so desirable as specimens for indoor gardens.

Creating a tropical environment
Plants form both the setting and the environment in a rain forest, and while it is obviously impossible to recreate tropical conditions in your living room, you can come close to providing optimum growing conditions by grouping warmth and humidity-loving plants together. Philodendrons, *Monstera*, *Scindapsus*, *Dieffenbachia*, *Adiantum*, some dracaenas, and many bromeliads make a luxuriant foliage display when grouped together, with some standing and others hanging. Still more ideal conditions can be provided for smaller plants in the controlled environment of a plant window or bottle garden, thus making a beautiful feature out of a practical necessity.

The desert environment
In complete contrast, are the growing patterns of plants in regions where conditions are anything but hospitable. Exposed situations, withering winds, drought, great heat and severe cold — any one of these factors might in itself be enough to discourage the easy colonization of plants. Taken together, as in the desert regions, it is a case of survival of those most able to adapt; self-sufficiency, rather than mutual dependency, becomes the criterion

Contrasting leaf shapes ◁
A stained glass window with a motif of sunshine and showers gently illuminates the delicate leaf forms of Adiantum *and* Plectranthus coleoides. *A* chlorophytum *arches protectively over the turtle doves.*

Grouping for texture and colour ▷
The restrained colours and smooth surfaces of the inanimate objects in this delightful grouping heighten the effectiveness of the choice of plants: Saintpaulia, *compact with velvety leaves and deep purple flowers,* Peperomia magnoliaefolia, *similar in leaf shape but greeny-gold and silvery, trailing* Sedum sieboldii.

for plant survival. Desert succulents have been forced to concentrate on the means of self-preservation and on economy of form in order to survive. In fact, these plants might almost have been fashioned by nature with the 20th century in mind, for the hot dry atmosphere of central heating suits them perfectly, and they are some of the easiest plants to grow in the home.

Special environments
Other groups of plants, such as the orchids, require conditions which are not necessarily difficult to achieve, but because they are so specific, they may not suit other plants. As a result, they tend to be grown in a special environment of their own. Purely from the point of view of design, the distinctive forms and growing habits of both succulents and orchids usually look best when grown in association with other species of their own kind.

Temperate environments
The large majority of house plants occupy the middle ground and are either, like many ferns and some palms, native to temperate regions or, like *Chlorophytum* and some *Tradescantia*, have proved themselves adaptable to a wide range of habitats and conditions. More often than not, they are also plants which grow in situations of shade or semi-shade, making them ideally suited to light conditions in the average home. In this range of plants can also be included some of those on the fringes of the more extreme groups which, for various reasons, have adapted to conditions outside those usual for their species. Many bromeliads, some orchids, the epiphytic forest cacti, some succulents and semi-succulents, such as *Yucca* will grow in average house plant conditions.

Most plants in this category will accept average to warm temperatures, with slight variations in either direction. As a result, they are the easiest to place in many different situations, and are the most suitable for arrangements that rely on diversity of form for their effect.

Matching character to design
All plants reflect, to a greater or lesser extent, their environmental conditions in their structural make-up. When grouping

is not pre-determined by specific cultural requirements, these specific characteristics, or features, can be used in a variety of ways and combinations for design purposes.

Some plants have one dominant trait — they might grow in an upright way, have variegated leaves, or produce flowers, for instance. Such individual characteristics can be used specifically to bring height or colour to an arrangement.

Other plants have several characteristics, which enable them to be used more flexibly, depending on the effect you want to achieve. *Scindapsus aureus*, for example, has variegated leaves and can be grown either as a climber or a trailer. Cane-stemmed begonias have variegated leaves, bear flowers and grow very tall, while *Spathiphyllum* is an attractive foliage plant for semi-shade, with the added bonus of arum-like flowers.

In some plants, a feature which tends to be characteristic of plants from a particular habitat can be used to suggest that habitat. *Cyperus*, for instance, with its many fine and slender stems is a typical waterside plant. Like the moisture-loving ferns, it looks wonderful when grown in this position (*see pp 72-5*), but can also be used in an arrangement to evoke the cool, tranquil atmosphere associated with water.

Personal taste and design
When planning any kind of plant grouping, you will naturally let your own ideas of what is pleasing influence the design. Once you have established that plants have the growing conditions they need to thrive, there is really no limit to the ways in which you can use their forms and qualities, either to blend and harmonize with the surroundings, or to contrast and surprise.

Choosing containers
Containers inevitably form an integral part of a group design, and so should be selected with care. If you are growing plants together in a single container, choose one which will complement the plants in terms of shape and colour, and also make sure that it is sufficiently large to accommodate the roots and spread of plants as they grow.

If you are using a piece of household china, or any other container which cannot be drilled with drainage holes, line the

bottom with a good layer of broken crocks, or gravel, to prevent water from settling in the soil. You will need to be rather more careful about the selection of plants grown in this way, since they must have similar soil and watering requirements if some are not to shrivel and others drown.

It is very tempting to include flowering plants in a container garden, but bear in mind that many are either outdoor, or cool conservatory, plants, which will rapidly wilt in warm rooms. Either use plants such as *Polyanthus*, *Streptocarpus*, and *Campanula isophylla* in temporary arrangements, or else

Matching plants to decor △
Themes from nature provide the inspiration for the decorative scheme of this room, from the printed wallpaper to the carved picture frame. No better setting for plants in an abundance of forms: Dracaena, Dieffenbachia, Aglaonema, Yucca, Aspidistra, Kentia *and* Scindapsus aureus.

grow them with smaller ferns and small-leaved ivies in a cool, bright spot, keeping the soil evenly moist. For colour in a warm-room group, grow the saintpaulias with humidity-loving pileas and *Pteris* ferns and add *Fittonia argyroneura* 'Nana' with its green and golden leaves as a ground cover.

HANGING GARDENS

From the simplest arrangement of hanging baskets framed in a window, to an entire room given over to a collection of the many plants that trail, creep or arch, plants grown in mid-air create visual surprise and dramatically open up the vertical dimension. The planting scheme can be as limited, or as ambitious, as space allows. Make the most of high-ceilinged rooms by introducing splashes of greenery and colour in otherwise dead space and by leaving the floor area free. If you suspend plants at different heights, you can cheat the eye cleverly by masking and softening the awkward proportions of a tall, narrow room, or a deep stairwell. Use plants with yellowy-green or variegated foliage to brighten and reflect the light and keep dark, heavy-leaved plants close to head-height to avoid making the arrangement appear top-heavy.

Creating a hanging jungle

Many of the plants best suited to being grown in hanging containers are forest epiphytes — plants that grow on branches in tropical rain forests — in light filtered down through the leaf canopy. Take full advantage of rooms with glazed roofs, or skylights, where the natural overhead illumination provides ideal conditions, giving an even distribution of light, and encouraging full, balanced growth. Here you can recreate a miniature hanging jungle, placing plants in their natural order — flowering bromeliads and forest cacti nearest the light source, with ferns and forest creepers, such as *Tradescantia* and *Ficus pumila*, protected by the leaves of the higher plants.

For an interesting variation in display, and a still more naturalistic effect, you can grow bromeliads and *Platycerium bifurcatum*, which actually attaches itself to bark or to moss and wire structures by means of the large, flat, sterile fronds at its base. Initially, however, it will need to be wired

Creating a window feature ▷
An elegant and supremely simple arrangement for the window of a town house. Innumerable star-shaped flowers of Campanula isophylla *'Alba', sparkling against dark green leaves, spill over the rim of a smooth white bowl. Chlorophytums arch gracefully on either side.*

Mixing hanging and standing plants ▽
Plants have been used to excellent effect here, where chlorophytum and variegated ivies bring animation and a sense of freshness to a setting busy with detail. Though it has great charm, the stained glass window reduces the strength of light, and affects the choice of plants accordingly.

on to the support, using moss as padding to avoid damaging the fronds. Attach bromeliads as described on pp 68-71. Water by unhooking and lowering both plant and support into a bath, or a bucket, of water — preferably rainwater.

A garden in your window
Where space, or light, is limited, a recessed window makes the perfect location for a more contained hanging garden, particularly if you want to screen, or distance, an unwanted view. If the amount of light is limited, choose only those plants with fine, light-coloured foliage. For a denser screen, grow taller, or climbing, plants on the sill to meet those cascading down, and in full-length windows place plants at floor level, or on a low shelf built across the window. This will help to provide humidity for the plants above.

Although it may seem paradoxical, a dark window can be wonderfully brightened by a collection of plants growing in amongst each other; if you are not getting much light anyway, it can be a very effective way of making a feature out of a disadvantage. The proximity of the light will allow you to include some variegated plants in the arrangement. The gold-splashed leaves of *Scindapsus aureus*, the silver markings of the Swedish ivy, *Plectranthus oertendahlii* 'Variegatus', even the humble *Tradescantia* in its mauve and silver varieties, will all add brightness to a green collection. The *Begonia rex* hybrids will make a striking diversion when grown in hanging containers, but their boldly-patterned leaves tend to dominate, so it is best to keep them at, or below, eye-level.

Temperature and humidity
A point to remember, when growing plants in heated rooms, is that warm air rises. As a result, hanging plants tend to dry out more quickly than plants at floor level and will need more frequent attention. However, always check the soil before watering,

47

since the rate of water absorption will vary. Although plants like *Chlorophytum* and *Tradescantia* will tolerate a certain amount of dryness in the soil and in the air, moisture-lovers like the ferns and bromeliads will rapidly show signs of distress if deprived of surrounding moisture for long, but will suffer equally if overwatered. This sensitivity can be countered by the use of compost containing a high proportion of moss-peat and some sharp sand, combined with frequent, even daily, misting. You can improve their immediate environment still further by suspending them over a group of standing plants, where they will benefit from moisture evaporation.

This technique has decorative, as well as practical applications. Several small ferns, or a single large *Nephrolepis*, can be grown over a group of taller plants to bring interest to a bare corner in a shaded room. Alternatively, by arranging plants in tiers on shelves built across the corner, or by staggering the heights of a group of plants, you can create the effect of a column of greenery rising from floor to ceiling.

Forming plant layers will also be the best way — and indeed may be the only way — to grow the more sensational trailers such as flowering *Aeschynanthus* and *Columnea* or the brilliantly variegated begonia vine, *Cissus discolor*. These prima donnas of the plant world are by no means easy to grow, requiring constant warmth and a high degree of humidity, but when grown amongst the plainer foliage trailers and suspended over a group of plants like philodendrons, which need similar levels of humidity, they make an arresting feature.

Choosing the containers

It is likely that your plants will be growing in many different types of container, but there is something to be said for continuity of effect, especially if plants are confined within a small area, or if you are growing one particular type of plant.

Cane hanging baskets come in a wide range of shapes and sizes and their textural quality makes them particularly well-suited to rooms where the emphasis is on colour and fabric. However, if they are to be practical as well as ornamental, they need to be made thoroughly watertight. You can line the interior with polythene sheeting

A miniature hanging jungle in your home　△
The extra space offered by an extension with a glazed and pitched roof has here been used to house a great variety of plants that intertwine in their profusion. Rhoicissus, Peperomia scandens, Chlorophytum,

tradescantias, Platycerium and philodendrons are easily grown species, but bromeliads and even an orchid flourish too, in good overhead light and where humidity is afforded by close grouping. Wrought-iron supports and a plaster column add elegance.

or, if the basket is large enough, you can place a plant saucer in the bottom. However, both these methods have disadvantages as, unless you remove the plant each time you water it, there is a danger that plants will be left standing in water. In addition, there may be seepage and consequent dripping.

Terracotta pots are the most decorative of all, but they should be securely fastened as they become very heavy when the compost is wet. Clay being porous, the rate of water absorption is faster, and plants will generally need more frequent watering. It may well be best to save terracotta pots for forest cacti and trailing succulents. Attractively decorated flat-backed wall pots can be used on the sides of recessed windows for bushy flowering trailers such as *Campanula isophylla* and small-leaved ivies.

Plastic containers, though less aesthetic, have the advantages of being light and easy to clean and are often made with a built-in saucer which prevents overflows. Tiered wire vegetable baskets are ideal for full-growing plants like *Asparagus sprengeri* which, grown one under the other, will in time form a hanging fountain of greenery.

Plant care

It is important to make sure that all the plants in your arrangement are easily accessible for watering and general care. If, however, the effect of your hanging garden depends for its success on having some plants beyond easy reach, then fix them on a weighted pulley system which will allow you to raise and lower them easily.

A hanging garden, perhaps more than any other form of plant display, needs to be composed of plants in peak condition. Because each plant in a group is seen in isolation, poor, unbalanced growth in one or two plants will ruin the overall effect. It is much better to be realistic at the outset and to grow only those plants which will adapt to available light conditions.

Do not let yourself be bound by convention — almost any plant can be grown in a hanging container, provided its form is not too upright. If a particular plant is thriving at floor level, you can achieve a most unexpected visual effect by repeating it at hanging level.

BOTTLE GARDENS

These miniature glasshouses make decorative features for just about any room in the home, from the bathroom to the living room, and they also provide the perfect answer to the problem of how to grow humidity-loving plants in a hot, dry atmosphere. While it cannot truthfully be said that they replace the full splendour of a warm conservatory, they do have the great virtues of being labour-saving and cheap to run, because, once established, they create their own self-supporting micro-climate. Moreover, if they are placed at eye-level on a table, or on a wide shelf, they will never fail to exert the undeniable fascination of an environment seen in miniature.

Gardens in bottles
It is technically possible to make a "bottle" garden out of any glass container, clear or tinted, as long as light can shine through the glass. However, some shapes are better suited to certain plants than others, either because of their ability to retain humidity, or because of their size.

The basic principle of the true, enclosed bottle garden is that once moisture is present within the container, it will be taken up by the plant roots and released in the form of water vapour, which, since it has no point of exit, condenses on the sides to trickle back down to the soil again. The narrower the opening or neck of the container, the more efficiently will this process be carried out; therefore the best shape for the real humidity-lovers is one which is full-bellied to allow quick run-off, with a narrow neck and base. This close humidity is well suited to small delicate plants such as *Fittonia argyroneura* 'Verschaffeltii', *Peperomia caperata* and the *Pteris* ferns.

Creating a miniature world

Although it may seem pretentious to talk about landscaping so small a feature, nonetheless, careful planning and arrangement of the plants will make the difference between a small work of art and a handful of plants in a bottle. You should also bear in mind that, once planted, rearrangement of a bottle garden is no simple matter. If you are using different plant families to represent a jungle microcosm, make full use of contrasting shapes to play tricks of scale and to heighten the illusion. As well as the naturally diminutive plants, you can use the larger, but slow-growing, varieties while they are still in their infancy. Palms are particularly useful in this respect, as their early form is a miniature replica of their mature shape, and they can be used to represent trees, standing above the bushier foliage plants. Small forms of *Codiaeum*, *Dizygotheca* and *Dracaena* will thrive in this

jungle, adding colour and variegation to the scheme. Bear in mind, however, that some plants will grow faster than others, and may eventually have to be removed, otherwise they will take over the garden.

Preparations for planting

Planting a bottle garden requires some dexterity and a great deal of patience. You will need a large funnel, a long-handled trowel and fork, a length of heavy-gauge wire with a loop at the end for lowering plants into the container, and a pair of tongs for moving plants around inside it. You can buy these implements, or you can improvise your own. Instead of the funnel, you can use a rolled-up sheet of paper; lengths of bamboo wired to a tablespoon and fork are good substitutes for the trowel and fork, and chopsticks, or lengths of cane, for the tongs. A cork on the end of a long skewer is ideal for tamping down the soil. A piece of cane with a sharp nail in one end makes a useful maintenance tool for picking up dead leaves and flowers. This tidying up process will be important, not just for aesthetic reasons, but to prevent

Desert in a jar ◁
Plants that need little attention but like steadily maintained environmental conditions are a good choice for bottle gardens – like this collection of cacti. Each one a conversation piece in its own right, under glass a careful composition of shapes unites to make a bizarre still life.

Wardian case gardens ▷
A stem of Dieffenbachia escapes from a latter-day Wardian case in which the plants enjoy constant ventilation without draughts. A rust-red kilim, equally reminiscent of 19th-century collector-travellers, provides an apt background.

the spread of fungal disease, which, if it takes hold, will spread all too rapidly in the warm, moist atmosphere.

Begin by washing out the containers scrupulously with warm water and ordinary detergent, or with a solution of vinegar and water, which should lift any stains. More stubborn marks can be dealt with, by using coarse salt as a scouring agent. Rinse thoroughly and allow to drain.

Once you are sure that the bottle is completely dry, use the funnel to pour a layer of sterilized and moistened gravel into the bottom. Follow this with a thin layer of charcoal chips to keep the soil sweet and then fill the bottle to about one third its volume with a soil-less compost. Shake the bottle gently until the compost is as level as possible, or, if you prefer, use the cork and skewer to contour it slightly. Now make a series of holes where you want to position the plants, taking care not to overcrowd them initially, because they will rapidly grow to fill the space in this ideal environment.

Planting

Lower plants one by one, using the wire loop, and manoeuvre them into position with the chopsticks. Bushy plants may need to be wrapped in paper to get them through the opening; the paper can be removed once they are safely inside. Alternatively, you can clip the plants slightly, as they will soon bush out again. Do not tamp down the soil until you have made sure that the arrangement looks good from all angles. It should have height in the middle and low-growing plants around the outside. When the plants are firmed in, add water slowly and gently through a narrow spout, letting it trickle down the sides. Then put the cork, or stopper, in place. Your aim should be to moisten the soil without saturating it.

The test will come in the first couple of days after planting when there should be no more than a light film of moisture on the inside of the bottle. If condensation is heavy, take the cork out and leave the bottle open for an hour or so until the moisture has cleared. However, if the sides of the bottle are dry, then add more water. Once the atmosphere inside has stabilized, the bottle garden will become virtually self-supporting, but keep a watchful eye on it. If

room temperatures have dropped recently, make sure that too much condensation does not build up. Containers should be kept out of the sun, in a position where they will receive light. Plants thus enclosed will survive for several years with little attention besides that already described.

Wardian cases

The discovery that plants would thrive in their own enclosed micro-climate was first developed commercially in the early 19th century by an English doctor, Nathaniel Ward. Originally, his plant containers were simple wooden and glass structures used for the transportation of plants, but they evolved into ornamental plant containers for the home. These structures, known as Wardian cases, were often on stands and had elaborate metal frames shaped into domes, hexagons, and miniature greenhouses with sloped roofs. Unfortunately, it is almost impossible to find one of these original Victorian designs, but their modern equivalent is the terrarium.

Terrariums

Terrariums, often made of acrylic, are available in a wide range of shapes, sizes and styles. The smaller varieties can be used to grow any of the miniature plants recommended for a bottle garden. A simple container, modelled on the idea of a bell-jar, might be used to display a single, spectacular, flowering bromeliad.

The larger the container, the greater your opportunities to expand by using the larger forms of *Croton, Dracaena, Aglaonema* and *Maranta*. A more subdued effect can be achieved by placing a collection of terrestrial bromeliads, such as *Cryptanthus*, in amongst moss-covered bark, planted with creeping *Ficus pumila*.

The Victorians used their cases mainly for ferns and these remain one of the very best choices of plant families for terrariums. The lush greenness of their foliage is at its most luxuriant when displayed in this closed environment and makes an extravagant complement to the linear structure of the container. Probably because they are so indelibly associated with the Victorian era, ferns tend to look best in old, or reproduction, cases.

If the idea of a plant container, which is both decorative and functional, appeals to you, then try making a plant table out of an acrylic container — square, rectangular or shaped like a giant bowl. If placed in a well-lit position and fitted with a clear top, it can be planted with colourful foliage and flowering plants to make a highly original feature. If the proposed location does not receive enough light, the table can be fitted with special fluorescent tubes and used to grow saintpaulias, and even orchids.

Planting these containers is simple in comparison with planting bottle gardens. Terrariums either have a door, a lid, or a detachable side panel. This makes it easy to remove dead leaves and flowers, or to extract any specimens that have grown too large or those that are ailing.

As the Victorians discovered, growing plants under glass can be both fascinating and extremely rewarding. The techniques required are described more fully in the chapters on plant windows (*see pp 60-3*) and conservatories (*see pp 38-41*).

Combining containers △
With a parlour palm for height, Ficus pumila at its foot and succulents for variety, this bottle garden forms the centrepiece of a pleasing symmetrical composition. In the bowl gardens the veined leaves of fittonias extend the range of plants.

PLANTS FOR BOTTLE GARDENS AND TERRARIUMS	
In small forms and for large plant cases	**Small-growing plants**
Aglaonema	Asplenium trichomanes
Calathea	Pteris ferns
Codiaeum	Selaginella apus
Ctenanthe	Sansevieria hahnii
Dieffenbachia	Peperomia caperata
Dizygotheca	Pilea
Chamaedorea elegans	Cryptanthus
Dracaena	Acorus gramineus pusillus
Maranta	Hedera (small-leaved kinds)
Saintpaulia	Pellionia pulchra
Asplenium nidus	Fittonia argyroneura
Adiantum capillus-veneris	Helxine soleirolii
	Ficus pumila

CACTI & SUCCULENTS

The desert landscape appeals greatly to some, to others not at all. At the furthest extreme of the range of succulent plants, the desert cacti, with their sparse and frequently outlandish appearance, have a definite curiosity value, which does not necessarily endear them to those who like their plants to have leaves. Nevertheless, it is difficult to resist the attractions of any plant which will flourish in the most inhospitable conditions with the minimum amount of attention, and yet continue to flower brilliantly year after year. Like the other succulents, many of which grow in conditions barely less extreme, these plants look best when grown in plain, unadorned settings which do not detract from the impact made by their unusual forms. Modern, or austerely furnished rooms, plain colours, and strong linear shapes provide a striking and appropriate context, which may be the closest you can come to evoking the lines and colours of a desert landscape in your living room.

Succulent or cacti?

The term "succulent" is used in broad terms to describe all those plants which — as a result of living in dry conditions — have developed the capacity for storing water in their leaves and stems. It is also used more specifically to distinguish between plants which bear areoles on their body surface and are known as cacti, and those which do not and are known as Succulents.

Areoles are small, cushion-like structures from which spring the veritable armoury of projections which characterize the cactus — tufts of hair, hooks, spines, barbed bristles and, of course, the sensational flowers. However, since the areole is not always visible to the naked eye, the true cacti can usually be recognized by their prominently swollen stems and lack of leaves. Although a few Succulents in the Euphorbia family can look confusingly like cacti, most either have succulent leaves and virtually no stems (*Agave*, for example) or branching stems and fleshy leaves (*Crassula*, for example). The forest-dwelling epiphytic cacti, however, are completely different in appearance, with pendulous branching stems, which are often mistaken for leaves.

It is important to decide whether a plant is a cactus or a succulent, so that you can give it the type of care it requires. Cacti prefer a combination of hot sun and moderate watering in summer, followed by bright, cool, or even cold, conditions and

KEY

1 *Opuntia cylindrica*
2 *Mammillaria magnimamma*
3 *Lobivia grandiflora*
4 *Notocactus leminghausii*
5 *Mammillaria bombycina*
6 *Opuntia rufida minor*
7 *Mutation of Chamaecereus silvestri grafted to Hylocereus*
8 *Opuntia graft*
9 *Cephalocereus senilis*
10 *Mammillaria hybrids grafted on to stock*
11 *Ferocactus townsendianus*
12 *Mammillaria hybrid*
13 *Notocactus claviceps*
14 *Deamia testudo*
15 *Echinopsis × greengold*
16 *Ripsalis virgata*
17 *Euphorbia obesa grafted on to stock*
18 *Mammillaria hybrid*
19 *Mammillaria elegans*

little or no water in the winter. With the exception of the desert varieties, Succulents prefer a slightly less severe regime, with some shading from very hot sun, more constant year-round temperatures and some water in winter. The epiphytic cacti should be treated more as ordinary house plants — placed in filtered sunlight, watered regularly and given a degree of humidity similar to that of their natural environment.

With the exception of the forest cacti, which adapt well to many different kinds of plant display, it is best to group succulents together since few other house plants will tolerate such extreme conditions. These plants positively revel in the hot, dry atmosphere of central heating and also enjoy being baked by the sun for several hours a day. Give them plenty of fresh air in fine weather, and keep them, as far as possible, cool and dry in winter. Overmoist atmospheres should be avoided at all costs

as the combination of conditions to which succulents are most likely to succumb is that of cold and damp.

Plants for miniature gardens

Succulents are slow-growing and, although many attain great heights in the wild, you can limit their growth still further by keeping them in small pots, thus restricting their roots. In this way, you should be able to avoid re-potting plants for as long as three years at a time. The familiar jade plant, *Crassula arborescens*, for instance, will grow into a small tree of up to 3m (10ft) in height. As a house plant, it is unlikely to ever top 1m (3ft), even in optimum conditions, and can be kept still smaller to make a charming feature for a miniature landscape.

In addition to these tall-growing plants, there are a host of naturally diminutive succulents, which are ideal for a small

container garden. They come in such a vast array of curious shapes and guises that it is impossible to do more than mention a few of the varieties which are easiest to grow in the home.

The many species of the *Mammillaria* and *Rebutia* cacti are all globe shaped and crowned during the summer with a succession of bright flowers in shades of pink, scarlet, yellow and white. They make a wonderfully colourful display, grouped

KEY

1   *Espostoa lanta*
2   *Ferocactus herrerae*
3   *Lobivia grandiflora*
4   *Graptoveria 'Victor Kane'*
5 & 6   *Opuntia bergeriana*
7   *Echinocereus engelmannii*
8   *Graptoveria 'Victor Kane'*
9   *Pilsocereus*
10   *Stetsonia*
11   *Dudleya pulverulenta*
12   *Pilsocereus*
13   *Ferocactus lamatacunthus*
14   *Pilsocereus palmeri*

together in a miniature dish garden and will not exceed 15cm (6in) in height. Smaller still are the *Gymnocalcium* cacti, which have flowers that are larger than the plants themselves. One of the most fascinating of the desert Succulents is *Lithops*. Known as living stones, they resemble small pebbles until they burst suddenly into flower, usually in the autumn. *Echeveria* and the smaller forms of *Aeonium* can be grouped to form a beautifully shaded composition in a small circular dish.

Choosing a container
The best containers are those which are shallow and wide. The root systems of these plants are small, so that depth of soil is not required; besides, there is always the danger that excess moisture will gather. A wide, open shape will encourage faster evaporation of water, as well as allowing greater surface reflection of heat around the plants. Containers may be of clay or plastic, although plastic is generally less attractive, particularly for group plantings. Plain terracotta, pottery with an interesting glaze or colour wash, an old china dish in blue and white, or plain white — any of these will complement the muted grey-greens of the Succulents, and avoid a violent clash of colours with the flowering cacti.

If you are using a container without drainage holes, you should line the bottom with a good layer of coarse crocks and gravel to absorb excess water. The growing medium should be one which warms rapidly in the sun, absorbs water readily and drains quickly and efficiently. Ready-mixed formulae are available, but you can make your own quite easily. Use a humus-rich potting compost as a base, with up to 30 per cent sharp sand or fine gravel; a little charcoal added to the mixture will help to counteract excessive acidity. The forest cacti, *Schlumbergera*, *Rhipsalidopsis* and the epiphyllums prefer a more moisture-retentive mixture; this simply involves adding some peat or leaf-mould to the base, and decreasing the proportion of sand.

Landscaping a succulent garden
Unlike the soft foliage plants that come from areas of luxuriant vegetation, where plants are all interdependent, succulents are individualists, designed by nature to

stand alone and to be self-sufficient in a more hostile environment. Take this into account when planning a succulent garden, and arrange plants to allow space between each; if you like, you can separate them literally with a surface sprinkling of fine gravel, or an attractive stone placed here and there. Not only will this make the arrangement appear more naturalistic, it will also improve the circulation of air around individual plants.

A wide windowsill can house a surprising number of succulents, so economical are their forms. Better still, where there is a sufficiently deep recess, you can unify the design by containing plants in a sealed and treated wooden tray constructed to the dimensions of the sill and to a depth of some 15cm (6in). Make a bed of small pebbles, or gravel, on which to rest the pots, and exercise your skills as a landscaper by introducing some interestingly-shaped large stones, or a piece of driftwood to break up the arrangement of pots.

A small succulent "alpine" garden makes an interesting variation on this theme. You can buy chunks of porous volcanic rock from some garden centres and specialist nurseries. The rock is drilled with holes to accommodate small species. Fill the holes and crevices with sand and an appropriate compost and plant them with small creeping sedums to trail attractively over the edge of the container.

Now plant the rest of the container with contrasting shapes, juxtaposing smooth, spherical forms with the deeply-ribbed bishop's hat cactus, *Astrophytum*, and the low-growing, clustering peanut cactus, *Chamaecereus*, with the upright, branching columns of the tall-growing *Cereus* species. Introduce foliage interest with the Succulent aloes and haworthias and break up the uniform appearance of the gravel bed by planting *Sempervivums* in scattered pockets of soil, so that they form colonies of small ground-hugging rosettes.

If the window behind your succulent garden is high enough, take the opportunity to grow some of the attractive, trailing succulents in hanging pots. The burro's tail, *Sedum morganianum*, the delightful string-of-beads, *Senecio rowleyanus* and the less-attractively-named rat's tail cactus, *Aporocactus flagelliformis* will all grow well in a sunny window and will counterbalance the windowsill garden below (*see also Plant Windows pp 60-3*)

Plant care

Although succulents certainly prefer neglect to over-attention, they require some basic care. During the growing season water plants well and then allow them to drain thoroughly. Do not water again until the soil is dry to the touch — the pot should sound hollow when tapped. Potting mixtures should always be well drained. A suitable mixture can be made by combining a good potting mix with grit, or coarse sand, and pieces of charcoal, broken grit or shingle. With this mixture there is no need to feed during the resting period, but during the growing season give plants regular feeds with a high-potassium fertilizer to assist flowering. In winter decrease watering and provide a drop in surrounding temperature. If this is not possible, at least move the flowering cacti to a colder spot and withhold water until spring. Later in the year you will be rewarded for this merciless treatment with a dazzling display of flowers.

Prickly companions △
The rotund shape of the golden barrel cactus,
Echinocactus grusonii, *contrasts pleasingly with the*
flat-jointed prickly pears, Opuntia microdasys.

Desert blooms ◁
The vivid pink flowers of Echinocactus scheeri *form*
a brilliant patch of colour in a mixed cacti grouping.
The Echinocereanae *make an ideal starting point for*
the novice, as they flower comparatively easily.

CACTI AND SUCCULENTS	
Cacti	**Succulents**
Astrophytum	Agave
Cephalocereus	Aloe
Chamaecereus	Conophytum
Cleistocactus	Crassula
Echinocactus	Echeveria
Echinocereus	Euphorbia
Echinopsis	Faucaria
Gymnocalcium	Fenestraria
Lobivia	Haworthia
Mammillaria	Kalanchoë
Notocactus	Lithops
Opuntia	Sansevieria
Parodia	Sedum
Rebutia	Sempervivum

PLANT WINDOWS

Creating a focal point △
Pride of place in this picture window with its pleasant view goes to an antique carving. Its slender lines are matched for interest by the divided leaves and delicate stems of Acer palmatum, *rarely grown inside, but which in full light will turn a glowing red in autumn.*

The area in and around a window is clearly a prime position for indoor plants, offering as it does optimum light conditions for a wide range of specimens. If there is no other part of the room where plants can be grown successfully, owing to poor light or to limited surface area, you can be sure that some plant will thrive in this location, whether it is a shade-loving fern or a sun-loving *Coleus*.

Assessing your windows
When planning a plant window there are some practical aspects that need to be considered, such as how the window opens, how often it needs to be opened and, most important of all, how much your own light supply will be diminished by the plants. If you plunge into creating a plant window without properly assessing its potential, you may find that what began as an attractive idea has in fact become an inconvenience; while from the plants' point of view, what began as a home may rapidly turn into an infirmary if they are constantly being moved or subjected to draughts and sudden fluctuations in temperature.

If a window is frequently in use, it should be kept as a display area for those plants that prefer cool conditions and enjoy some ventilation. It is also suitable for plants which flower for short periods.

If your view is less than desirable, plants offer an excellent way of creating a feature which concentrates attention on the interior. If, on the other hand, the window overlooks a garden, or has some other attractive view, you may prefer to keep planting to a restricted height.

Types of window
If the outlook provides the setting, it is the dimension of the window itself which ultimately will define the limits of your arrangement, as well as determining whether the plants become integrated with

the rest of the room or make a separate feature that is set back from the room.

Bay windows and recessed windows can be fitted with shelves to make a separate display area. The extra depth provides the opportunity to create an arrangement which is fully three-dimensional and will make a beautiful focal point in a room which has no other plants. Painted latticework, fixed to the sides and across the top, will not only look extremely decorative, but will also provide support for climbing plants and a means of hanging containers on hooks.

If your window is flush with the wall and does not have a particularly noteworthy frame, it can be adapted to form a recessed window, by building a wooden frame out and around it. Although it may at first look rather odd in relation to the rest of the room, you can get over this by using every inch of space to create a concentrated display of flowers and foliage which will draw attention away from the underlying structure.

Large picture windows need little other ornament than a few well-chosen specimen plants to break up the expanse of glass and to provide some foreground. If more disguise is required, clear glass shelving, fitted right across the window, will support a collection of variegated and flowering plants without blocking too much light or making an abrupt visual interruption. Make sure that you choose containers that are in keeping with this effect.

Light

The quality, amount and intensity of light that enters a room quite naturally plays a part in defining its character. Windows automatically draw the eye towards them and plants in these areas are supremely placed to capture and reflect the light, or lack of it. For this reason, it is important to plan carefully both the type and the arrangement of any window plants. Although the range of plants that can be grown successfully will be partly dependent on temperatures within the room, you will find that, unless the window is very small or overshadowed, the very proximity of the light will enable you to grow many more plants here than in a position even a short distance from the window.

Positioning plants △
This window arrangement is successful from a design point of view, with its attractive combination of upright, bold-leaved plants and arching or trailing forms. The effect is complemented by the choice of containers and a variety of interesting knick-knacks. However, the plants will not thrive unless they receive some shading from direct sunlight.

Certainly there are plants that need full sun, just as there are plants that must have shade, but in between there are many variegated and flowering plants whose dependency is on light, rather than direct sun for colour and bud formation. Depending on the temperature, ivies, tradescantias, *Maranta*, *Begonia rex*, flowering *Impatiens* and *Campanula isophylla* can all be used to enliven an arrangement that is predominantly green.

However, the green of plants is never uniform, and there is much to be said for a shady window which is lavishly planted with a collection of ferns. Use the variation in green and the many frond shapes to create interest, then add moisture-loving plants such as *Cyperus* to the arrangement. *Cyperus*, standing in a bowl of water, will help maintain the level of humidity, while pots of *Helxine* and mossy *Selaginella* will add the finishing touches to a lovely, tranquil scheme which needs no further colour to enhance it.

At the other end of the light spectrum, a small window that receives direct sunlight for several hours a day will make an ideal home for tiny cacti. As well as being trouble-free and easy to grow, many species will flower profusely all summer long, and then continue to provide interest with their curious shapes and forms.

A quite startling effect can be achieved in a large window by including in your arrangement some of the larger cacti, and the beautiful grey-green succulents, whose colour provides an excellent foil for the brilliance of the cactus flowers. Balance the whole scheme by suspending trailing succulents and lovely forest cacti overhead, in simple terracotta containers. These plants need little but the plainest of settings to give maximum effect. White walls and frames, simple containers, and some filtering of very strong sunlight in the form of a white Venetian blind, will combine to make a highly arresting display.

A recessed window that is both warm and bright can be adapted to house a collection of colourful tropical plants, which, because of their demands for good light and a consistently-balanced micro-climate, may be difficult to grow elsewhere in the home. By creating a specialized environment within the confines of the window recess, rather like a miniature hothouse, you will be able to grow a wide variety of unusual foliage and flowering plants, ranging from *Codiaeum* and *Caladium* to flowering bromeliads, and even orchids.

Temperature and the feature window
A feature window requires careful planning and attention to detail, backed up by scrupulous maintenance, if it is to remain in peak condition.

The room itself needs to be warm — it is best if temperatures are not allowed to fall below 18°C (65°F), as severe fluctuations of temperature will result in foliage drop. However, if you ensure that the window itself is proofed against the outside weather, and has the means to maintain its own equilibrium, you should be able to avoid having to live in hothouse conditions.

It is obviously important that the plant window should not be your only source of ventilation; it will need to be carefully sealed against draughts, and well protected from frosts in the winter months. Double glazing that can be opened in warm weather is the ideal solution, but a temporary

second skin in the form of a glazed frame, or clear vinyl sheeting, that can be taken out in summer and replaced as the weather gets colder will do just as well. A light screen or blind may be necessary to shade plants from intense sun.

A nearby heater will help to direct and localize the temperature, but since humidity is the crucial factor for these plants, dry air should be countered by the use of some kind of humidifying device such as a large bowl of water or a water tray, which hooks over the side of a radiator. If you are intending to grow rare and expensive plants, then it is probably worth investing in a small, electrically-operated room humidifier. The tropical plant window can be made all the more self-sufficient by the simple addition of a moveable glazed front, either in the form of a sliding "door", or a second window which opens outwards (*see pp 38-41*). Whichever method you choose, much of the guesswork can be eliminated by the use of a hygrometer. This instrument measures and indicates the exact degree of humidity in the atmosphere. Placed in the window among the plants, it enables you to monitor and regulate the humidity level.

Plants will benefit enormously if they are grouped together in shallow trays, or containers, lined with a layer of gravel, or pebbles, kept constantly moist. Make sure, however, that pots are never standing directly in water. In tall and full-length windows, plant arrangements will be most effective if shelving is well spaced to allow good air circulation around the plants. Slatted shelves will increase air circulation as well as letting in more light and permitting moisture to percolate upwards to the higher plants that are in most danger of becoming dry. It is also most important to give individual plants room to spread, as overcrowding in warm, moist conditions can lead to rotting. Any dead, or damaged, plant material should be removed immediately to prevent disease.

Concealing an unattractive view ▷
Columns of greenery mask an unwanted view without blocking light from the upper half of a picture window. A huge Dieffenbachia *soars impressively above a philodendron and a* Rhoicissus rhomboidea, *while a fine specimen of green-leaved* Tradescantia albiflora *cascades over a terracotta column.*

ORCHIDS

An orchid window is, without doubt, one of the most beautiful and, quite literally, breath-taking features of an indoor garden. In fact, if you were to grow only orchids in your home — as many people do once the passion for them has taken hold — you would have a display of exquisite colour and almost endless variety from winter through to spring. However, even if your interest never carries you to these extremes, you can make a most effective small feature within a recessed window, by including both standing and hanging orchids and using as a theme, several species from the same genus, or those with flowers in many variations of a single colour.

An abundance of choice

The bewildering problem at first is where to begin when faced with a family of plants that has such a diversity of cultural requirements, and at least 20,000 different species. The answer lies in the wide distribution of their habitats, which range from tropical jungle to Arctic tundra. Some orchids grow in sultry, swampy ground, others at high altitudes on misty mountain tops. There are some 750 classified genera, roughly half of which are epiphytic, growing on the trunks and branches of trees, the other half terrestrial, growing in the ground. Even within the comparative limitations of a forest eco-system, there are some epiphytic species which grow high up above the tree canopy, where they are bathed in warm light and air, while others grow close to the forest floor, in shaded and more humid conditions.

Following these natural divisions of climate and topography, genera are usefully divided into three groups — cool, intermediate and warm-growing. Of the three, the cool and intermediate types will be best suited to indoor cultivation in temperate climates. It is also generally accepted that the beginner will find it easier to grow epiphytic species rather than terrestrials. The warm-growing varieties, such as the *Vanda* group, usually need higher levels of heat and humidity than can comfortably be provided outside a warm greenhouse, or heated conservatory.

It is worth obtaining a good grower's catalogue, which lists the many species and hybrids available, with details on individual forms, sizes, flower colours and flowering periods. Even within a single genus, individual species differ enormously in size and appearance — some are evergreen, some deciduous, some robust and upright, others arching and slender, some grow to 1.8m (6ft) and more in height, others no more than 15cm (6in), while the flowers come in just about every known colour.

Creating a suitable environment

Success with orchids depends on a balanced combination of four factors: light, the appropriate temperature, humidity and ventilation. While levels of temperature, humidity and ventilation will vary according to the group, you must be certain that you can provide all orchids with a position in good light, preferably one which

Contrasts in colour △
*Earthy reds, browns and green are typical of many of
the wild species orchids with forest origins. Each one
striking in its own way, they make a stunning display
when grouped together, showing between them a
variety of extravagantly intricate details, veins
and markings.*

Striped beauty ◁
*Cultivated hybrid orchids like these bear blooms of
such perfection they need to be studied at close hand
to be fully appreciated. The depth of colour, the
immaculate whiteness and the development in form
from promising bud to extraordinary flower together
exercise a unique fascination.*

receives several hours of sun a day. The
best position, if you are beginning with two
or three plants, will be the windowsill with
the warmest aspect. Some plants, however,
will require more shading than others and
you will need a light, slatted, or Venetian,
blind, that will filter sun for those that
need it, and give protection to others at the
hottest times of the day. If you only have a
window which receives morning sun, you
may have to consider supplementing
natural with artificial light to provide an
ideal 10-12 hours of daylight during the
period of maximum growth and flowering.
Plants in the cool-growing group need

Orchid opulence ◁
An exotic collection using all hues of pink, with white, as the unifying colour theme where all else is variety: orchids that differ in height and habit of growth, some flowers appearing to cascade downwards on the stem like a waterfall, others with frivolously frilled petals.

daytime temperatures of 16-21°C (60-70°F), while those in the intermediate group prefer temperatures of 18-24°C (65-75°F). Provision must also be made for a drop of 5-8°C (10-15°F) at night. If plants do not have this natural resting period they will over-expend their energy and will show signs of weak growth and reduced flowering. This drop in temperature tends to occur quite naturally in rooms which are centrally-heated only during the day. However, if you are in any doubt, use a room thermometer.

Humidity and ventilation go hand in hand for orchids, which is not surprising when you consider that many of these plants grow on branches, where they are simultaneously bathed in warm moisture from surrounding foliage, and dried by the air circulating round them. This continuous process is very important, and you can help to provide the right conditions by standing plants on upturned pots in shallow trays of moist gravel. Make sure that the plants are well above the water level. A hygrometer placed among the plants is a very useful way of checking that conditions are consistently maintained — most plants in the cool to intermediate range prefer humidity levels of between 40 and 60 per cent. An open window nearby will help to keep the air moving in mild weather, though cold draughts are to be avoided. Orchids dislike stuffiness as much as humans; an electric

fan will improve conditions for both you and your plants when days are very warm and still. All plants will benefit enormously from a spell outside in summer. If you are growing plants in either internal or external plant windows (*see pp 60-3 and pp 38-41*), the best arrangement will be one which uses well-spaced slatted shelving to increase the circulation of air.

Some epiphytes will adapt quite happily to being grown in pots, others look and grow best when mounted more naturalistically on slabs of cork and bark. To do this, wrap damp sphagnum moss around the roots and wire the plant on to the support, which can then be suspended on a length of wire, or nylon thread.

Orchids in pots
For pot-grown plants, you can choose between plastic or clay containers. Plastic pots have the virtue of being light, but they retain moisture and therefore tend to become sweaty; while this is ideal for many house plants, most orchid growers favour clay pots because they are porous, and provide a cooler and drier environment for the roots. Clay containers are often available with perforations around the sides, which allow air to get in and the roots to wander. These pots and the delightful, slatted, wooden, hanging baskets, which can be filled with damp sphagnum moss and used for some epiphytic

species, together make a beautiful display, well suited to the airy quality of the tree-growing orchids.

As you might guess, the growing-medium needed for pot-grown orchids is quite different from the conventional compost used for other house plants. The basic constituent must be one which is light, free-draining and allows roots maximum ventilation. Osmunda fibre is the traditional material, but owing to scarcity and the high cost, it has been superseded by shredded fir-tree bark, either on its own or mixed with moss-peat and vermiculite. Terrestrial species will normally require a mixture that contains higher proportions of water-retaining moss-peat.

Orchid care

The rule with watering — and this applies particularly to the epiphytes — is water and drain thoroughly, then leave plants until the compost is on the verge of becoming dry, before watering again. One of the features which distinguishes the dryer-growing orchids from the more conventional types, is the presence of one, or more, swollen stems at the base. These pseudobulbs, as they are known, are used as storage vessels for water and nutrients, and plants that have this ability to reserve moisture do not need such frequent watering as those with fleshy roots only. In fact, overwatering can prevent the pseudobulbs from functioning correctly.

All plants need more frequent attention during the growing and flowering seasons, but it is always a good idea to test below the surface of the pot before watering — the compost may still be wet, even though the surface is dry. Plants on moss and bark will need still more frequent watering — they can be lowered into a bucket of water (rainwater whenever possible) and then hung up again to dry.

Many orchids have a resting period after flowering, and during this time there will be little, if any, evidence of growth. Reduce watering and only increase the amount as signs of new growth appear. If you are not using any form of mechanical humidifier, mist plants daily, or more frequently, if necessary. Like watering, misting is best done in the daylight hours, so that plants have time to dry out before the temperature drops.

All this may sound complicated, but you will find, over a period of time, that you are able to judge, by the feel of the compost or by the sound of a pot when tapped, whether the plants need to be watered either more or less. Their requirements will vary from week to week, according to temperatures inside and outside the room.

In every other respect, tend orchids as you would any indoor plant. Remove dead leaves and flowers to prevent the spread of disease. Any failure to thrive or flower is more likely to be caused by some imbalance in the growing conditions, rather than by a viral affliction, though these can certainly arise if plants are left for too long in unsatisfactory conditions. Fertilize plants regularly during the growing season, using the prescribed amount of a special orchid fertilizer. Fertilizing must not be neglected, particularly in the case of plants growing in fir-bark, or vermiculite-based, composts, which have no, or few, nutrients. Turn pot plants regularly to ensure that all parts of the plant are receiving light as evenly as possible. The gentle current of air provided by an old-fashioned ceiling fan will help to rotate the higher-growing hanging plants.

Individual perfection ▽
The large, pure white and deep mauve flowers of Laeliocattleya 'Amacynth' usually appear in autumn or winter and last for two or three weeks.

BROMELIADS

Although these fascinating plants are found only in Central and South America, their range of habitats is extremely diverse. The result is a family that includes what must be some of the world's most spectacular foliage and flowering plants, as well as some of the strangest, most unplant-like forms in existence.

A strange and wonderful plant
Bromeliads fall into three categories: those which are epiphytic, and grow on trees; those which are terrestrial; and, most curious of all, the xerophytic, or atmospheric, bromeliads, which derive their nourishment solely from the atmosphere. The unique form and growing habits of these air plants — which all belong to the genus *Tillandsia* — put them in a category apart, since they alone cannot be grown in soil.

The distinguishing feature of the bromeliads is their leaves — often marked and banded in contrasting colours, or etched with intricate tracery designs; some so tiny as to be virtually indistinguishable from mosses and lichens, others huge, fleshy and strap-shaped, but always, and invariably, arranged spirally to form a rosette. In many species the central leaves of the rosette form a vase with a watertight base which acts as a reservoir for collecting rainwater, and the nutritive detritus of fallen leaves and small insect life.

As if the leaves were not in themselves sufficient reason for growing these beautiful plants, many species also produce brilliantly coloured flowering heads, either on tall stems, or within the heart of the rosette. The flower itself is usually small and often relatively insignificant in comparison with the surrounding bracts which remain brightly coloured for months on end.

Flaming sword △
Vriesia splendens *revels in the common name
Flaming Sword. Those of the species which have
beautifully marked and patterned leaves make a
valuable contribution to a collection of bromeliads,
where they contrast well with plain-leaved varieties as
well as providing height and an elegant silhouette.*

Brilliant bromeliads ◁
*Guzmanias in flower are a compelling sight, inviting
the eye to a glowing centre of vivid scarlet or orange.
They should be placed where they can be seen from
above for the form to be appreciated. After flowering
the plant dies, but offshoots appear at the base which
can be detached and potted up.*

Since it is the leaves which provide the plants with vital nourishment, the root system has little function other than to anchor the plant to its support. It is, in consequence, comparatively small. Plants grown in pots seldom need to be moved on, unless the rosette has grown so large that it is in danger of overbalancing.

Bromeliads for all occasions
Contrary to expectation, these exotic plants are not necessarily difficult to grow. They need good light, with filtering from strong sun, to maintain the leaf colour, average to warm temperatures of around 16°C (60°F) throughout the year and a certain amount of humidity. Most will grow quite happily in normal home conditions. Their easy disposition and independence of spirit make bromeliads enormously versatile, and, as a result, extremely adaptable to different forms of display — from hanging baskets and dish gardens in the case of the more conventionally-growing kinds, to simple ornamental mounts for the dry-growing *Tillandsia*.

An epiphyte that falls from its perch in the forest will frequently simply resume life as a terrestrial. This means that most of the epiphytic bromeliads also make very successful pot plants, provided they are grown in a medium which is both absorbent and free-draining. Excessive moisture around the roots and base of the rosette will quickly lead to rotting. The ideal mixture consists of high proportions of peat, sphagnum moss, or leaf-mould, and some coarse sand to assist drainage.

Bromeliad trees
Undoubtedly the most appropriate, and indeed the most spectacular, way to grow bromeliads is on a bromeliad tree. Depending on the size of the room and on the scale of your ambitions, this can be an attractive piece of driftwood mounted on a stand, or a small branch suspended from the ceiling, or part of a small tree cemented, in a vertical, or semi-horizontal position, into a strong base, such as a piece of tree trunk, or a stone trough.

Whatever the scale, the basic principles of construction are the same. Firstly, that the means of attachment, whether to a base, or to a hook, must be secure;

secondly, that the piece of wood must be strong enough to bear the plants.

Once the tree is secured, wrap damp sphagnum moss tightly around the branches and fasten it in position with fine wire. If the plants have been growing in pots, ensure that their roots are entirely free of soil, wrap the root ball in more damp sphagnum moss, then wire that to the branches. Nylon stocking makes a good alternative to wire, as it will not damage the plants, nor will it rot.

When choosing plants for a bromeliad tree, you may need to use the resources of a specialist nursery to obtain some of the less readily available species. Aim to make a display which is balanced in effect, both literally in terms of weight and size, and in the contrast between coloured, patterned and plain leaves. The overall effect should be striking, but not overdone. *Tillandsia*, with their charmingly detailed and tangled leaves, will mute the brighter colours with pale greys and soft grey-greens. The rootless Spanish moss, *T. usneoides*, in particular, makes a delightful contrast to strong shapes with its many minute strands forming moss-like tufts that can be draped over the branches here and there.

A bromeliad tree will need frequent spraying, particularly when conditions are hot and dry, and, as this can be rather a damp operation, it is a good idea to spread newspaper on the floor around large trees. The aim should be to mist around the plants, rather than to drench them. Whenever possible, misting should be done in the early morning and never in bright sunlight.

Plant care

Larger bromeliads with a water vase, such as *Aechmea*, should have their vase filled, preferably with rainwater. The vase must be topped up from time to time, particularly in high temperatures and when plants are in flower and the rate of water absorption is faster. Keep the moss around root balls damp, but not sodden. Smaller arrangements can be lowered occasionally into a bath of water, but remember the purpose is to moisten rather than to soak. These same rules of humidity apply to plants grown in pots. It is a good idea to stand the pots in an outer container packed

with damp sphagnum moss, while keeping the compost just moist.

One important point to note about flowering bromeliads, is that the onset of flowering also marks the death of the main rosette. The plants, however, are continually renewing themselves, and, at around the same time, will produce small offsets at the base; these should be left in place until their size is about two-thirds that of the parent. The original rosette can be cut away gradually as it begins to show definite signs of dying back. Because the dying process is so slow as to be barely discernible, it will not spoil the effect of the display. It is, therefore, important to resist the temptation of detaching the offsets until they are properly developed, and can then be potted on, or reset on the tree. Bringing new plants into flower is rather more difficult, since high temperatures of at least 29°C (84°F) are required, but, since the foliage is in itself so decorative, it will not matter if it is impossible to provide these conditions.

Mixed groups

The smaller terrestrial bromeliads can be displayed in a shallow container with other small plants that like similar conditions. Half fill a wide, flat-bottomed dish, or tray, with a suitable soil mixture (*see epiphytic bromeliads*). Place a piece of thick bark, or driftwood, on this base, and then cover the bark, either partially or entirely, with sphagnum moss. Wire the moss to the bark or wood. Next, wire the moss-wrapped root balls of the plants on to the bark, or plant them shallowly in the compost.

Most simply of all, air plants can be mounted on shells, coral, sculpted wood or stone, by means of a special fixative (which can be bought at nurseries or garden centres), or hung from a thread as a mobile. Mist them gently from time to time.

Creating a bromeliad tree △
One of the best ways of displaying bromeliads together is on a "bromeliad tree". Even if it is not possible to maintain sufficiently high temperatures to bring new plants, like this Neoregelia carolinae, *into flower, the variegation of vriesias, cryptanthus and other neoregelias among the plain green can make for a display of rich diversity. Much of the beauty of these plants lies in their sculptured shape; each one of them demands attention.*

BROMELIADS	
Large bromeliads – to 60cm (2ft) – suitable for bromeliad trees or pot culture	**Small-growing and terrestrial bromeliads**
Aechmea fasciata	Neoregelia ampullacea
A. 'Foster's Favourite'	N. 'Red of Rio'
Billbergia nutans	Cryptanthus fosterianus
Guzmania lingulata	C. bivittatus
G. zahnii	C. zonatus
Ananas comosus	Cryptogergia rubra
'Variegatus' (ornamental	
pineapple)	**Air plants**
Vriesia splendens	Tillandsia caput-medusae
V. fenestralis	T. bulbosa
V. hieroglyphica	T. tenuifolia
Neoregelia carolinae	T. argentea
Tillandsia lindeniana	T. recurvata
Nidularium innocentii	T. usneoides
	T. tricolor
	T. ionantha

WATER GARDENS

Water gardens can be just as attractive indoors as outdoors. If you have sufficient space and there is enough natural light, such a feature can be a real talking point, providing a striking contrast to the other elements in your overall indoor garden design. Bringing water into the home in this way provides both visual relief and a sense of vitality. Given the right conditions, creating a water garden also enables you to simulate a sense of the tropics indoors.

Positioning your pool

Ideally an indoor pool should receive a high level of warm, natural light and should have at least some overhead glazing. If you want to grow aquatic lilies this is essential, as these beautiful plants need full light and sun to grow and flower successfully.

Conservatories and glazed extensions make perfect sites for water gardens, not just because of their large windows and skylights, but also because they are likely to have tiled or vinyl flooring, which is impervious to damp and will not be damaged by spillage.

If the pool is to be simply a water feature with no plants, light is less important and the pool can be positioned for maximum impact, or to separate one area from another. In small rooms, with restricted light, a well-positioned mirror will double the effect and also throw back reflections. If you add a small fountain, the movement of water will more than compensate for any lack of natural light, particularly if the pool is lit from beneath.

If you are planning to build a pool in a carpeted room, it is advisable to tile the area around the pool and also to raise the pool above floor level. For safety reasons, such rooms should be put out of bounds for small, unaccompanied children.

Designing the pool

A design based on nature is unlikely to be completely successful in an indoor setting, as it will require more space than is normally available within the average room. However, you might consider looking to the ornamental pools of the Islamic world for inspiration. Built in many shapes from marble, stone or brightly

Planting a small pool ◁
Nymphaea 'Blue Beauty' is a tropical hybrid suitable for a small heated pool or tub. The spectacular blooms, which open in the morning and close up in the late afternoon, deserve a situation where they can be enjoyed at close quarters.

Creating an exotic pool ▷
The margins of this warm pool are enlivened by the colour and variegation of bromeliads, coleus, stromanthes and scindapsus, all of which benefit from constant warm humidity. Cyperus rises gracefully from the centre of the pool to provide an impressive focal point.

patterned tiles, they often had fountains and were unadorned by plants. Another feature which you can borrow from the Islamic garden, is the narrow water channel, flanked by formal planting in pots. This will make a very effective feature in a cool conservatory or a long garden room.

The shape you choose should be appropriate, both in scale and design, to the dimensions and character of the room. The most attractive, and indeed the most practical, design for a small pool, is one which is raised to a height of some 46cm (18in) above floor level, with a rim that is wide enough for seating and for pots. The smaller the pool, the more important it is to keep the design simple; the area of water should always be more prominent than the pool's surround.

If you are about to add an extension to your home, you will be in an ideal position to design the pool as an integral part of the room, using a concrete construction, edged with brick, or clad with tiles. Pre-formed, resin-bonded glass fibre pools can be obtained from garden centres and will slot easily into an opening in the floor. Alternatively, if you want the pool raised, it should be supported in a treated timber frame. In either event, it is better to choose simple geometric, rather than so-called "natural", shapes. A useful feature of glass fibre pools is that they are often made with ledges at the sides to accommodate shallow-growing aquatic plants.

Whichever method you choose, make sure that the construction, or housing, is absolutely watertight, and also that there is an outlet for the water which connects directly to the main drain. If the pool does not have an outlet, you will have to bail it out each time the water needs changing. A new concrete pool should be "cured". This means that it should be filled and left to stand for a week. The pool should then be emptied and the process repeated once more. Finally, scrub the pool with a vinegar and water solution. This procedure helps to get rid of alkaline exudations; the pool can then be painted with a non-toxic fish-pond paint, and planted up.

Heating
The next decision is whether to heat the pool or not. You will certainly not be restricted in your choice of planting material if the pool is warmed by solar heat alone, for any of the hardy nymphaeas and other aquatic plants for the outdoor water garden will grow very well indoors; they may even grow more vigorously under the added protection of glass. However, if your interest lies in the tropical plant species and exotic fish, then the water should be heated to a constant average temperature of 21°C (70°F). Some species will grow in temperatures of 27°C (80°F), but plants and tropical fish will suffer if the temperature drops below 18°C (65°F). Thermostatically-controlled immersion heaters are available from garden centres and aquarium stockists.

If you wish to illuminate your pool, use low-level underwater lights, which add a pleasant glow without confusing the fish.

Tropical touch ◁
A jungle pool in a tropical glasshouse owes much of its effect to dense planting in beds around the water's edge, where ferns and tall cyperus make a lush backdrop for colourful bromeliads and nymphaeas.

Choosing the plants

Aquatic plants basically fall into four categories and each has a role to play in maintaining the conditions vital to a healthy and well-balanced water habitat. *Nymphaea*, and the related *Nelumbo*, have underwater stems and roots, but their leaves and flowers float on the surface. They differ widely in size, some requiring a greater depth and surface area of water than others. The miniature, and small-growing, *Nymphaea*, that grow in depths of 15-30cm (6-12in), are the best choice for a small, ornamental pool.

The floating aquatics absorb all the nutrients they need from salts in the water. Although less spectacular than the flowering lilies, they include many flowering and foliage plants, which will grace the pool surface. By shading the water with their leaves, the floating aquatics help to prevent the formation of that colonizer of still water, blanket weed, as well as providing food and protection for fish.

The submerged aquatics live entirely beneath the surface, where the gentle swaying of their finely-divided leaves brings movement to the water. They are also invaluable as "oxygenators", helping to keep the water clear, and absorbing the carbon dioxide emitted by fish.

The fourth group includes many plants with diverse forms, some with floating leaves and flowers, some with long stems, which will trail over the pool edge and others, such as *Cyperus papyrus*, or

C. alternifolius, which send their long grassy stems up to 1.8m (6ft) above the water surface. All are soil-rooted and many will grow in water 15cm (6in) deep, or less, and so are ideally suited to very shallow pools, or to ledges close to the surface.

Despite this great wealth of choice, it is best to resist the temptation to overplant; not only because overplanting can overwhelm a small pool, but also because, if too great a part of the surface area is shaded by foliage, it will cause problems for both fish and underwater plants.

Planting floating and submerged aquatics is simple enough – the first are just placed on the water, the second will probably need to be weighted down with a small weight, or lead clip. Water-lilies, however, and other soil-rooting aquatics must be planted. The usual method is to grow them in special perforated polythene baskets filled with good loamy soil and a little organic fertilizer, such as bonemeal. The best time to plant lilies is in the spring, and since they need to be gradually acclimatized, you should start by supporting the baskets on bricks to within 15cm (6in) of the surface. Gradually lower them to the bottom as the plants become established — a process which generally takes about six weeks.

With or without aquatic planting, a small, lightly-shaded pool in a warm room can be made to seem still more mysterious by surrounding it with humidity-loving plants that will benefit from the moist atmosphere. Philodendrons, palms, *Ficus* and ferns will help to mask the pool edges with their foliage. Hanging orchids and bromeliads, placed close to the light source, will add vibrant colour and transform your water garden into a secret retreat — a tropical forest pool.

AQUATICS FOR UNHEATED POOLS
Nymphaea odorata minor
N. laydekeri lilacea
N. laydekeri purpurata
N. 'Graziella'
N. pygmaea 'Helvola'
Azolla caroliniana (floating)
Hydrocharis morsus-ranae (floating)
Eliocharis acicularis (submerged)
Myriophyllum prismatum (submerged)
Vallisneria spiralis (submerged)

AQUATICS FOR HEATED POOLS
Nymphaea stellata
N. 'Mrs G. H. Pring'
Eichornia crassipes major (floating)
Pistia stratiotes (floating)
Ludwigia mulertii (submerged)
Salvinia braziliensis (floating)
Vallisneria torta (submerged)
Myriophyllum proserpinacoides
Limnocharis humboldtii (shallow/ledge)
Cyperus papyrus (shallow/ledge)

INDOORS/OUTDOORS

Climate inevitably influences both house and garden design. It also affects the way people view the areas around their houses. In warm climates, gardens, verandas, patios and steps all become natural extensions of the home. In colder climates, the outside world becomes a picture seen through the windows. However, whether these "halfway" areas are in frequent use, or whether they are merely viewed from inside, they provide the immediate context for your home. Strong, imaginative planting will do much to enliven them and to bridge the gap between the indoor and the outdoor world.

City gardens

This link between the indoors and the outdoors is particularly important in cities, where the smallest garden, balcony or windowsill is of especial value as a means of putting some distance between you and your surroundings, and also of extending your indoor garden.

One way of transforming a small city garden into an extension of your home, is to exchange the traditional patch of lawn and surrounding flowerbeds for a more formal arrangement of paving and plants in pots. Particularly when connected to the main living areas by glazed doors, these outside rooms make delightful retreats for sitting and eating out in the summer months and provide interesting views of evergreen shrubs and climbers, stone pots and ornaments in the winter.

Such areas are usually very sheltered, and are ideal for growing plants which are midway between being tender and fully hardy. If there is one wall which receives direct sunlight, save it for growing flowering wall shrubs, such as *Acacia dealbata* (mimosa), *Abutilon megapotamicum* and *Fremontia californica*.

Here too, you can keep those tender plants, such as *Pelargonium*, which need to be taken in if there is any danger of frost,

but which will otherwise benefit from being outdoors. The trailing pelargoniums and pendulous, bedding fuchsias make colourful displays in pots and hanging baskets; pale blue *Plumbago capensis*, grown with white and soft pink petunias adds coolness and serenity. The less hardy jasmines, *J. polyanthum* and *J. primulinum*, bring fragrance to sheltered corners, which receive some sun.

Use these enclosed areas to rest indoor plants, such as *Azalea indica*, *Cyclamen persicum* and *Schlumbergera* × 'Buckleyi', which have flowered in winter and need sheltered conditions to ensure that they flower the following season. Many other indoor plants will enjoy a short break outside and an occasional bath in warm summer rain, but plants with dark, glossy and waxy foliage should be kept right out of the sun, otherwise their leaves will become bleached and scorched.

Courtyards

The most unprepossessing space, if it is enclosed by walls, can be transformed by painting the walls white and by adding a paved, or tiled, floor. In tiny areas it is best to choose paving units to suit the scale: brick, laid to a basketwork, or parquet, design, and gravel (pea shingle) are both warm, textural materials, which look equally good separately or combined. Either will add a note of formality.

In sunny and sheltered spots you can conjure up an Italian courtyard, with citrus trees in terracotta pots, arranged formally on a raised platform where they can be seen from inside. The Chusan palm, *Trachycarpus fortunei*, adds a most exotic flavour, eventually reaching a height of 3m (10ft) if planted directly in the ground. Although it is slow-growing, you may prefer to restrict its growth by keeping it in a large pot.

Fatsia japonica and × *Fatshedera lizei* are handsome architectural plants that

Country charm △
A full-length window is transformed by colourful pelargoniums and daisies arranged on zinc gravel trays supported by shelf brackets. The otherwise unattractive glazing bars are hidden from view and the choice of terracotta pots forms part of the simple arrangement, complementing the countrified air of the room. Pelargoniums like plenty of sunshine and will benefit from the extra ventilation provided when the sliding door is open.

Room with a view ▷
This sun-dappled courtyard is both an extension of the home and a pleasing view in its own right. Bamboo and other evergreen planting combine with the mellow warmth of brick to give a lush yet tranquil atmosphere. Sculptured birds are objects of beauty with permanent appeal, while seasonal interest comes from flowering plants such as azaleas.

associate well with paving and hard
surfaces. They look most striking in simple,
rather modernistic, settings, where their
large, fingered leaves make bold patterns
against the plain background. These plants,
as well as *Camellia*, *Arundinaria* (bamboo)
and the many ivies, all make excellent pot
plants, and have the added virtues of being
fully evergreen and shade-tolerant.

Even the smallest enclosed space will
acquire a certain romance if it can be
designed to accommodate running water
somewhere within it. Fountains do not
have to be grandiose, or even expensive,
items — the simplest kind consists of a
small self-circulating pump, which can be
installed in a pre-cast concrete container
and run off the main electricity supply.
This makes a delightful centrepiece for
a small courtyard, or an atrium. A water
feature is also a particularly useful way of
enlivening dull and overshadowed areas

Living in a garden △
*The division between house and garden is almost
indetectable in this courtyard living room, where the
lush planting of* Arundinaria, *palms, hanging baskets
of* Asparagus sprengeri *and trailing ferns disguises
walls and doors and then merges with the garden
beyond.*

where nothing much will grow. You can
turn the view of a gloomy yard, or well,
into a visual surprise by installing a wall-
mounted basin fountain, and surrounding it
with containers of ferns and bamboo.

Balconies and window ledges
You are less likely to be beset by problems
of light if you live above ground level in an
apartment, but, unless you have access to a
garden, your outside growing space may be
restricted to a balcony, or a window ledge.
In the narrowest of spaces, where only a
window box or a long trough will fit, you
can establish an evergreen background of

trailing ivies and small-growing junipers, and then add an ever-changing display of seasonal bedding plants and bulbs.

A window ledge that is not polluted by traffic fumes makes a good home for a collection of herbs, mixed with miniature bulbs such as *Muscari, Eranthis, Iris reticulata* and dwarf narcissi. All these plants like a light free-draining soil, and plenty of sun. With a little ingenuity, you can persuade all sorts of unexpected plants to grow in such a limited space. For instance, if there is room for a deep box, you can fill it with a good compost, enriched with some well-rotted manure, and grow dwarf runner beans, or sweet peas, on canes, to form a most attractive summer screen. A more formal, but highly original, arrangement can be composed by combining neat, round, ornamental cabbages, in shades of mauve, pink and white, and the silver-green, spreading form of *Ballota pseudo-dictamnus*. The latter is a very attractively-leaved plant, which provides a perfect foil for the pink and purple shades of plants such as petunias.

If there is enough space, a balcony can be planted more permanently, with a framework of evergreen and flowering climbers trained on wires or trellis. Once again, ivies are the obvious answer, but you can also try clematis, honeysuckle, jasmine and *Passiflora caerulea*. Some of the smaller climbing roses are suitable for pot culture, but, like all pot-grown plants, they need to be fed regularly, and, preferably, mulched, if they are to give best results.

Unfortunately, balconies and window ledges can be very exposed, and plants may be battered by the wind, unless they can be given some form of protection. Balconies with glass, or solid fronts, offer shelter for the lower plants growing within their lee. Extra protection can be given to taller plants, by fixing a strip of trellis across the top of the ledge and using it to support climbers such as the semi-evergreen honeysuckles, which are generally reasonably wind-resistant.

A sunny balcony can be filled with colour from top to bottom, by growing plants like lacecap hydrangeas and annual climbers such as *Ipomoea* (morning glory), *Thunbergia alata* and *Cobaea scandens*. The latter is actually a perennial, but is unlikely to survive the winter if temperatures drop below 5-8°C (40-46°F). *Campsis radicans*, a flamboyant climber with orange-scarlet, trumpet-shaped flowers, needs a warm, well-protected position, where it will adhere to its support with self-clinging aerial roots.

Formal balconies with wrought-iron railings look best with rather controlled planting. Small clipped bay trees make lovely feature plants — either alone, where their dark, glossy leaves provide year-round relief from concrete and stone, or as a background for vividly-coloured summer planting. Bay will not tolerate too much exposure, but an equally charming topiary feature can be made for less sheltered positions, with the slower-growing dense-leaved box, *Buxus sempervirens*.

Plant care

As with any form of container growing, these plants need frequent and regular attention, which can easily be overlooked just because they are out of the way. It is important to remember that it is not only sun which dries plants out, wind can have an equally devastating effect, even when temperatures are cool.

Ensure that all containers are properly drained, and remove excess water from pot saucers after watering. From a purely neighbourly point of view, if you are living several stories up, make sure that you have some way of containing overflows. Always use a special-formula sterilized compost, rather than garden soil which may contain weeds and bacteria. Feed shrubs and climbers about once a fortnight in the growing season, using only the prescribed amount.

Apart from watering and feeding, it is also important to examine your plants from time to time to check for signs of pests such as aphids, which can wreak havoc unless severely dealt with; once established, you will probably find that you have to treat them at least once a week, either by spraying with plain water, special aphid killer, or, better still, by the painstaking, but effective, finger and thumb method. For the longest possible flowering display, deadhead flowering plants regularly throughout the summer, and when they are over, fill in the gaps with bulbs.

SCREENS

The modern trend towards open-plan living undoubtedly allows for a more flexible use of space and, therefore, more freedom of movement within it. However, the pressure of living constantly in this way can be a strain — there seems to be a primitive desire in most people for areas that are both secluded and private. This is presumably why, in large open-plan offices, and industrial buildings that have been converted into homes, the old divisions reappear in the form of partitions, half walls and screens. In these situations, plants offer a solution which is at once more interesting, and more flexible, than a solid partition; a foliage screen can make an effective room-divider, and, at the same time, be a decorative feature in its own right.

Simple screens
At its simplest level, a plant screen can be composed of a group of plants informally arranged so as to mark the junction between one area and another, or to mask an unwanted view; the screen remains fluid, in that individual plants can be moved at any time, to alter the shape of the group and change its effect.

Where greater definition is called for, and to make a permanent division between two areas, plants can be used in combination with a simple frame. A constructed screen immediately formalizes an arrangement by defining the shape that the planting takes, and there are many plants with a climbing, or twining, habit, as well as tall-growing plants with flexible stems, which adapt very well to this type of planted screen. You can use them, according to their shape and size, to suit a variety of different situations.

As with any plant arrangement, it is important to suit the scale of the plant to the scale of the room. A screen of large-leaved, climbing philodendrons look overpowering in a small space, but make a magnificent and highly effective room divider in a large, open-plan area. These sturdy plants, with their handsome, arrow-shaped leaves, stout stems and prominent, fleshy, aerial shoots give a strong sculptural effect as well as a dense cover, up to 1.5m (5ft) in height.

A simple structure can be made to support the plants by fixing vertical posts at intervals to a piece of wood, sawn to the required length and screwed to the floor. These plants like a high degree of humidity, so, for the best results, treat the timber in advance with a damp sealant. Once the frame has been constructed, wrap damp sphagnum moss around the posts and wire it into place — in this way you will encourage the aerial shoots to adhere to the structure and, eventually, to cover it. A more enclosed effect can be obtained by fixing a second piece of wood across the top of the frame and growing flexible-stemmed *P. scandens* around the entire structure.

In a large, high-ceilinged studio, you can extend the framework upwards, and then use the lateral timbers for suspending hanging plants. If the display is not too far from a window, vividly flowering bromeliads and the gloriously coloured begonia vine, *Cissus discolor*, climbing or trailing among ferns and other trailing creepers, will create a sensational effect, particularly if dramatically lit at night. These large-leaved plants, such as *Tetrastigma voinierianum* and × *Fatshedera lizei* look best on this rather rudimentary type of structure, but the smaller-leaved climbers need more delicate frames — both to set them off and to allow them to twine.

Trellis screens
Lightweight garden, or ready-painted indoor trellis can be used without modification, or it can be cut to a variety of shapes, including rounded or gothic arches. Where you want to make an enclosed corner, rather than a flat screen, two panels

Creating room-dividers ◁
Rhoicissus rhomboidea *clambering abundantly over trellis work provides a welcome note of colour and texture in an office – a living screen that effectively breaks up the open plan to furnish more private work-spaces.*

can be fastened together at right angles. For this kind of ornamental frame, choose plants with simple foliage and plain green leaves, especially if the screen is painted. Two vines, in particular, will make a rapid and attractive cover — *Cissus antarctica* and *Rhoicissus rhomboidea*. Both are vigorous climbers with attractive glossy green foliage; *Cissus* is the taller of the two, but *Rhoicissus* is more spreading. As the plants grow, tie them loosely to the trellis at intervals, using plastic-coated wire, or green garden ties. Both climbers prefer average to cool conditions and partial shade. Grow sinuous *Jasminum polyanthum* among them to provide a contrast in leaf shape and size. Green and variegated ivies — either the small-leaved *Hedera helix* varieties or large-leaved *Hedera canariensis* – will give a delightfully fresh garden air to a screen in a cool area. Ivy-leaved *Senecio macroglossus* 'Variegatus' will give a similar effect in warmer locations, and can be grown with the taller *Scindapsus aureus* to form a colourfully variegated screen.

Containers
When growing plants against any kind

of framework, it is inevitable that the containers will intrude to some extent. The most obvious solution, when growing plants in a line, is to use a rectangular container of the same length as the frame. Wooden containers look best, but need to be treated inside and out to prevent seepage and rotting. They should be raised slightly off the floor, and be fitted with a drip-tray underneath. This can be concealed by a fascia board fitted flush with the floor.

An all-in-one construction, that will do away with the problem of separate containers, can be made from a rectangular, or square, wooden box and three pieces of wood. Nail two upright pieces to the middle of the inner sides at either end of the box, then attach a horizontal piece across the top to form a three-sided frame. Wires, or narrow laths, can be fixed across the frame — vertically, horizontally or diagonally — and, for added flexibility, the whole container can be mounted on castors. The main advantage of this scheme is that plants can be grown on both sides of the frame, making a screen which looks equally good when viewed from either side.

If you prefer to keep plants in separate

containers, then use square, rather than round pots, for these will fit better against the screen. In order to avoid having a bare strip of trellis showing at the bottom, cut away the piece in between the pots, so that it is in line with the pot tops. Glazed ceramic pots in clear strong colours can look very effective, particularly if the screen is painted.

Room dividers

Long rooms, particularly when serving a dual function as both living room and kitchen, are often fitted with a divider in the form of a built-in unit, a low cupboard, or open shelving. These surfaces can be adapted to provide a foliage screen, which can be used to conceal the kitchen from the sitting area without disrupting the sense of visual continuity.

Depending on the style of the room and on how high, or dense, you want the planting to be, there are a number of tall-growing foliage and flowering plants that will be ideal for this purpose. Room dividers are usually equidistant from windows at either end, and thus tend to be in areas of relatively low light. One of the most striking of the tall-growing plant families actually prefers indirect light — the colourful begonias. The tall, cane-stemmed varieties will reach an eventual height of 1.2-1.8m (4-6ft) and offer a dazzling array of foliage, ranging in colour from deep red, brown and purple to olive green and silver, with striking patterns and markings. All these plants produce clusters of pink, or coral, flowers in spring and summer.

In a narrow area, open shelving can be constructed at right angles to the wall and taken as high as the proportions of the room permit. In wider spaces, a free-standing unit can be built up to ceiling height in the centre of the room, allowing space for a passage on either side. Constructions such as this look most effective if shelves are arranged at different heights, so that taller and climbing plants can be grown as a contrast to smaller-growing forms. A bright-leaved climber, such as *Scindapsus*, is best grown near the bottom, where it will climb up into the light, and not overbalance the scheme. Contrast upright shapes with arching and cascading forms, and introduce points of detail, with plants like *Ficus pumila*, *Pellaea rotundifolia* and *Helxine*, amongst the rounded forms of Boston ferns and *Tolmeia*. Experiment by moving plants around until you can see where a striking shape like that of *Platycerium bifurcatum* is needed, and where a note of colour can be added in the form of a flowering, or variegated, plant. For a more uniform effect, use only feathery leaves, rounded shapes and trailing forms; in this way the pots will be hidden, giving the illusion of a curtain of greenery.

Plant care

Any arrangement, which is as prominently on display as a planted screen, needs careful planning and regular attention. It is of the utmost importance to choose only those plants which will grow effectively in the prevailing conditions — this includes light as well as temperature. Provide moss-sticks for those plants that need humidity, and ensure that they are always kept moist. Make sure that all containers are properly drained, so that plants are never permitted to stand in water.

It is inevitable that plants growing together in a permanent position will at times look less than dazzling, particularly in winter, but regular removal of dead and damaged foliage, and pinching out the growing tips of strongly growing climbers will prevent them from becoming straggly.

Check regularly for aphids and red spider mites in dry and hot conditions, and treat plants as soon as you detect any sign of these pests. If one plant is particularly badly afflicted, it is better to be ruthless and remove it, rather than to risk the trouble spreading to the other plants. Regular spraying will help to keep pests and disease at bay, and also to prevent dust from gathering.

Masking an unwanted view ◁
The noise and bustle of a busy main road have here been effectively screened from view by a collection of plants that thrive in a west-facing window, so arranged to admit ample light to the room. The deep recess houses a delicate Asparagus sprengeri at the top, contrasting with the dramatic fronds of stag's horn fern at centre left. Rhoicissus rhomboidea climbs upward from floor level to mingle with cyperus and its fellows on the sill.

INDOOR GARDENS

Plants play a vital part in people's lives. Sadly, it is often only in their absence that it is appreciated how greatly plants improve an environment. Nowhere is this more evident than in cities, where green space has given way to increasingly large areas of brick and concrete, and there is little visual relief from hard surfaces. Now, however, planners and architects are beginning again to correct the balance, and to reintroduce planting in some new and dramatic ways.

City gardens

Surely one of the most curious manifestations of 20th century urban life must be the experience of walking along a street, which has barely a trace of natural vegetation and catching a glimpse of an office interior which is teeming with tropical plant life. An awareness of the increasing need to humanize the scale and material of large buildings has brought about the introduction of the indoor garden as a most welcome feature in the entrance halls of offices, hotels and apartment blocks. These oases of greenery bring much-needed visual and sensory relief to those who work or live among them, and, though they are clearly far beyond the scope of the average indoor gardener, they can be a most useful point of reference for less grandiose schemes in your office or home.

Much of the impact of these magnificent show-pieces comes from the sheer scale and extent of the planting. However, you are likely to recognize the familiar shapes of *Ficus benjamina*, *F. lyrata*, *Araucaria excelsa* and the various palms. Wherever the ceiling height allows, you will be able to use large specimens of these plants to similar effect, creating a canopy that encloses an area, but still allows a view through it.

Planning the garden

In the domestic context, you will obviously be dealing with areas considerably smaller than these, but the considerations of scale in relation to space will still apply. For this reason, the most appropriate and effective place to site an indoor garden in the home is an area open in design and well-lit from the sides (preferably from above as well). Spacious open-plan rooms and entrance halls, enclosed atriums or glazed extensions are all excellent choices, as they allow maximum visual impact and give the plants the room they need to grow freely.

Large or small, the planning of an indoor garden, whether for the office or the home, must take into account certain basic considerations: how to make the best use of the available space, how to combine decoration with function, choosing plants to suit the existing light levels, screening without causing obstruction, and plant maintenance.

Oasis of greenery ◁
Spreading branches and a carpet of greenery soften the bare, functional lines of this modern office. The combination of tall and low forms provides visual variety and creates an impression of space and light.

Creating a living room garden △
Strong design and imaginative planting prove that an interior garden can be as successful in the home as in the office. Plants of different heights and varying leaf *shape have been grouped skilfully around a small pool to form an indoor garden that complements the simplicity of the decor, as well as providing a focus of interest.*

The obvious advantage that the professional has over the amateur gardener, is in the means and resources available. The area of glass in a modern office is often vast, and even then can be supplemented by special Plant-Gro lights. Costly, and highly sophisticated equipment can be installed to take care of watering and maintain the correct humidity levels. Full-grown trees can be imported, and contractors employed to clean, tidy and replace. However, do not let this dampen your enthusiasm. The huge advantage that you, the home gardener, have over the professional, is that the garden is yours, and your plants are unlikely to be subjected to anything like the same wear and tear, or to be used as receptacles for litter. If you have chosen your plants with care in the beginning, and continue to treat them with consistency, you have every right to expect them to flourish and, furthermore, to live far longer than they do in an office scheme.

Design and construction

Once you have decided on the position of your indoor garden, the next step will be to decide whether it is to be a moveable feast or a permanent feature. Depending on the size and function of the area, and on the kind of effect that you want to create, there are many different design approaches you can adopt.

Large planters or hydroponic units offer a solution that does not necessitate any structural alterations. If mounted on castors, they can be moved easily and relocated if you want a change, or if plants outgrow their position. If, however, you prefer the idea of an indoor garden that is more naturalistic in effect, there is no reason why you should not think about making a planting bed in the floor. There is no doubt that it is a great deal easier to combine plants of different forms and growing habits when they are growing among each other, uninhibited by pots.

Plants in seats ▷
Raised plant beds transform an ordinary bench into a pleasant place to sit and relax. The arching branches of the palms provide an impression of shade and foliage without being overpowering.

Simplicity of effect ◁
Uncomplicated plant designs are often the most effective. Trailing plants soften the strong vertical lines of this all-white office, while the single large specimen plant balances the overhead arrangement. A cleverly-placed mirror enhances the atmosphere of sunlit serenity.

Most architects dealing with large-scale planting for commercial buildings, will make provision for it at the planning stage. If you are building a new home, or adding an extension, you will be able to do the same. It will be important to have, in advance, a pretty clear idea of which plants you want to grow, since it may well influence the dimensions, and even the shape of the bed itself.

Both in design terms, and for practical reasons, it is usually best to position a planting bed centrally, away from walls.

Not only does this allow the arrangement to be seen from all sides, but it makes maintenance easier and eliminates the possibility of damp spreading into the wall and upwards. If the bed is to be constructed at the same time as the building, then it will be a simple enough operation to have a recess built into the floor which is lined on all sides, but lets down into the foundation rubble. This will allow water to drain naturally away from the plants and the building.

If the bed is a later addition, you can

make the recess in the floor to the required dimensions, and then form a sunken container from concrete poured *in situ*. The particular advantage of poured concrete is that it allows you flexibility in the choice of shape. More limiting in this respect, is the use of a pre-formed container, such as one of the fibreglass shells used for pools (*see pp 72-5*). Stainless steel is another option – it is expensive, but highly durable. If the bed is contained rather than opening down to the foundations, then you will need to line it well with broken bricks and rubble for drainage.

It is most important to choose suitable material for the adjacent flooring, something which will not be damaged by water spilt or dripping from the foliage. Slate, marble, terazzo, quarry tiles, concrete or vinyl are all suitable. Wood floors must be close-fitted tongue and groove and be properly sealed.

Raised beds
Where the space is large enough to take the visual interruption, raised planting beds can be a useful way of keeping plants out of a passageway, marking a change in level, or adding interest to an awkward corner. However they need to be most carefully

Variety and balance ◁

Blessed with an abundance of windows and light, this office is defined by its plants. A huge Ficus lyrata dominates the arrangement, while the smaller dracaena, philodendrons and schefflera provide both balance and variety.

on the strength and intensity of light the garden receives. Assuming it is in a position to receive maximum exposure to light, the arrangement will be a matter of personal taste and suitability for the position.

As with any kind of group planting, the best results will come from a skilful association of forms, colours and textures. Bear in mind that there are some areas that will benefit from bright colours, while others are more suited to a predominantly green mass of foliage. In rooms or areas where there is little competition from furnishings or decoration, the red of *Cordyline terminalis* 'Firebrand' and the bright, volcanic colours of the crotons look extremely dramatic. However, these and other brightly coloured or variegated plants will stimulate rather than relax the eye. So in living areas where a more tranquil atmosphere is needed, it is probably best to choose plants with more muted colours instead, or to harmonize the group by using plants of similar form but of different heights. In this respect, dracaenas make excellent companions. Tall-grown specimens can be bought, several metres in height; single or multi-stemmed, they make maximum impact with the minimum amount of fussiness or intrusion.

Where space allows, there is much to be said for the sheer simplicity of a single splendid tree, standing quite alone. For this purpose, the deservedly popular *Ficus benjamina*, available in heights up to 10m (30ft), could hardly be bettered for the grace and serenity it creates. Another exquisitely graceful plant for a smaller space is *Dizygotheca elegantissima*. But you must be certain that you can maintain a high and consistent degree of humidity to keep it in good condition.

The space around an open-plan staircase is often underused, but in fact, it provides a group of tall-growing plants, such as *Philodendron erubescens* or the large-leaved *Ficus lyrata*, with an excellent position. These can be grouped together in

planted, if the bare edges and sides are not to appear more noticeable than the planting itself.

Choosing the plants

Having decided on the best way to contain your indoor garden, you can now set about bringing it to fruition. If you are growing plants in a permanent bed, it is more than ever important to suit the plants to the context, and to each other. It will not help the plants to settle down and grow vigorously, if they are being constantly lifted and changed around. The choice of planting, as always, will depend mainly

containers, or planted in a small bed to one side of the staircase, and grown with other smaller, and more spreading forms at the base.

One of the most positive practical aspects of growing large numbers of plants together is that it is generally far easier to achieve stable conditions, and thus minimize maintenance. Most plants will grow better and more vigorously because they are able to benefit from the collective humidity.

Probably the chief reserve most people have about doing anything on a large scale is the possibility of wholesale and expensive failure. Certainly, the glory will be yours if you are successful, but a failure can be at best a ghastly eyesore, at worst a costly mistake. If you are investing in really large plants, be sure to buy them only from a reputable nursery or plant stockist, who is prepared to give you advice on how best to acclimatize the plant. It is sometimes safer, if you are uncertain as to whether or not you can provide the right conditions, to opt for a smaller plant that is more able to adapt as it grows.

It is equally important to choose plants to suit your lifestyle. If you know that you will be unable to spend at least an hour a day tending temperamental plants, spraying and regulating humidity levels, then choose, initially at least, plants that are less demanding. As time goes on, you will probably feel more confident about adding some of the more temperamental specimens.

It will not really matter if circumstances force you to choose only the most familiar plants, because the truth is that every plant is beautiful when it is in the peak of health. Often the simplest schemes are the most successful, so you should never disregard the possibility of using those plants you know to be reliable in less-than-perfect conditions, just because they seem ordinary or unexciting. In the end, anything you read is best taken only as a useful guideline, because nothing can replace your own enthusiasm and willingness to experiment and sometimes take risks.

Height and space ◁
Planting on a grand scale transforms this central courtyard into a haven for office workers. Equally pleasing effects can be achieved in the home, provided there are high ceilings. Keep the decor and furnishings simple and use arching, graceful plants, such as Ficus benjamina *and palms.*

The tranquillity of water ▷
A serene pool, bubbling fountains and lush planting refresh the spirit and provide a soothing diversion from the bustle of city life. This indoor water garden can be used as a model for a similar feature in the home, using more domestic materials such as warm brick, or colourful tiles.

DESIGN GUIDE

These quick reference tables condense the information given in the first section to enable you to select the plants best suited to your particular decorative requirements. Plants are grouped according to their growing habits – climbing, creeping, trailing and hanging – and average height – low, low-medium, medium and tall. Each plant is then described in terms of appearance and its possible design applications.

CLIMBERS

Plant	Application	Impression of foliage/form	Flower
Asparagus plumosus	Group backdrop	Fine, feathery	
Bougainvillea	Heated conservatory	Papery, showy	
Cissus antarctica	Screen, vertical emphasis	Vigorous	
Cissus discolor	Bright colour in group	Vibrant	
Cissus striata	Screen, group	Delicate, tangly	
× Fatshedera lizei	Screen, group	Sturdy, handsome	
Ficus pumila	Column, group	Dainty	
Hedera	Screen, group	Cool dense	
Hoya carnosa	Screen, feature	Waxy, elegant	Yes
Jasminum	Heated conservatory, feature, screen	Delicate, graceful	Yes
Monstera	Screen	Glossy, architectural	
Peperomia scandens	Group interest for screen	Bright, detail	
Philodendron scandens	Screens, group planting	Vigorous, fleshy	
Plumbago	Cool conservatory	Cool, light	Yes
Rhoicissus	Screen, vertical emphasis	Exuberant, leafy	
Scindapsus	Colour in group, screen	Fleshy	
Senecio macroglossus	Accent for screen	Bright, ivy-like	
Stephanotis	Flowering feature, heated conservatory	Fleshy, exotic	Yes
Syngonium	Screen, feature	Cool, handsome	
Tetrastigma	Screen, vertical emphasis	Cool, handsome	

CREEPING TRAILING HANGING

Plant	Application	Impression of foliage/form	Flower
Asparagus sprengeri	Hanging garden, plant pedestal	Feathery, cascading	
Bromeliads	Hanging garden, plant window	Variegated rosettes	Yes
Campanula	Hanging garden	Tumbling	Yes
Ceropegia	Detail in hanging garden	Charming, miniature	
Chlorophytum	Hanging garden, plant pedestal	Grassy, arching	
Cissus striata	Hanging garden	Delicate, tangly	
Columnea	Heated conservatory	Trailing column	Yes
Davallia	Hanging garden, shaded fern window	Feathery, furry rhizomes	
Epiphyllum	Flowering feature, hanging garden	Succulent, branching	Yes
Ficus pumila	Detail in hanging garden	Dainty	
Fittonia	Humid dish garden, terrarium	Bright detail	
Gynura	Hanging garden	Purple, hairy foliage	
Hedera	Foil in hanging garden, cool conservatory	Cool, dense	
Helxine	Ground cover group	Dainty miniature	
Hemigraphis	Colour in hanging garden	Metallic, trailing	
Hoya bella	Flowering detail in hanging garden, heated conservatory	Graceful, arching	Yes
Hypocryta	Flowering feature, hanging garden	Detail, trailing	Yes
Nephrolepis	Plant pedestal, hanging garden	Frilly, dense	
Orchids	Humid hanging garden, heated conservatory	Diverse forms	Yes
Pellaea	Detail in hanging garden, group	Arching, miniature	
Philodendron scandens	Hanging garden	Vigorous, fleshy	
Pilea nummularifolia	Detail in hanging garden, group	Tumbling	
Platycerium	Hanging garden	Sculptural	
Rhoicissus	Hanging garden	Exuberant leafy	
Saxifraga	Hanging garden	Trailing detail	Yes
Sedum morganianum	Hanging feature, succulent window	Pendulous succulent	
Selaginella	Terrarium	Mossy, feathery	
Tolmeia	Hanging garden	Soft mound	
Tradescantia	Hanging garden	Bright, trailing	

LOW

Plant	Application	Impression of foliage/form	Flower
Adiantum	Terrarium, humid plant window	Fine, lacy	
Asplenium	Feature, shaded fern window	Fresh, glossy	
Begonia rex	Colour in group	Showy	
Coleus	Bright window, colour in group	Warm, colourful	
Ctenanthe	Shaded plant window, terrarium	Cool, subtle	
Cyrtomium	Lightly-shaded group	Glossy, holly-like	
Hypoestes	Colour in group	Detail	
Maranta	Humid plant window, group	Muted colour	
Pilea cadierei	Group interest	Metallic	
Pteris	Bottle garden, small humid dish garden	Charming, detail	
Rhipsalidopsis	Flowering feature	Succulent, branching	Yes
Rhoeo	Feature	Wide tapering rosette	Yes
Schlumbergera	Flowering feature	Branching, succulent	Yes
Stromanthe	Humid plant window, variegation in group	Subtle colour	

LOW-MEDIUM

Plant	Application	Impression of foliage/form	Flower
Aglaonema	Group, shaded area	Cool, variegated	
Aspidistra	Plant pedestal, feature for shade	Upright, dark	
Caladium	Tropical plant window	Colourful, translucent	
Calathea	Humid shaded plant window	Subtle, elegant	
Chamaerops	Feature	Dense, fan shape	
Codiaeum	Tropical plant window, focus	Exotic, glossy	
Cordyline	Tropical plant window	Colourful accent	
Cycas	Feature	Stout, feathery, tufted	
Hydrangea	Cool conservatory, flowering feature	Robust, showy	Yes
Microcoelum	Feature	Feathery, open fan	
Orchids	Humid plant window, heated conservatory	Diverse forms	Yes

Platycerium	Feature	Sculptural	
Sansevieria	Desert garden, feature	Upright, severe	
Sparmannia	Cool conservatory, feature	Open, light	Yes
Spathiphyllum	Accent for group	Dark, slender, graceful	Yes

MEDIUM

Plant	Application	Impression of foliage/form	Flower
Araucaria	Feature for cool shade	Dark, tiered	
Chamaedorea	Feature	Elegant	
Coffea	Feature	Shrubby, glossy	
Dieffenbachia	Feature, group	Sturdy, bright	
Dizygotheca	Feature, tropical plant window	Fragile, elegant	
Fatsia	Feature, cool conservatory	Handsome, architectural	
Ficus lyrata	Feature, group	Sturdy, handsome	
Gardenia	Flowering, feature	Fleshy, exotic	Yes
Rhapis	Feature	Slender, elegant	
Yucca	Feature, group	Upright, spiky	

TALL

Plant	Application	Impression of foliage/form	Flower
Abutilon	Cool conservatory, indoors/outdoors	Large, light	Yes
Beaucarnea	Feature	Tassled, curious	
Begonia × 'Lucerna'	Screens, group	Bold, colourful	Yes
Ficus benjamina	Feature, group	Graceful, arching	
Ficus elastica	Feature, group	Dark, robust	
Heptapleurum	Feature, group	Upright, detail	
Howea	Feature	Elegant	
Monstera	Feature, group	Glossy, architectural	
Phoenix	Feature, group	Elegant, spiny	
Schefflera	Feature, group	Radiating, handsome	

PART TWO

THE A-Z OF HOUSE PLANTS

SELECTING PLANTS

The success of your indoor garden depends on the quality of the plants that you select.
It is worth taking the time to examine plants carefully before you purchase them. If you
have spent a great deal of time and thought selecting suitable plants, nothing will be more
disappointing, nor more likely to undermine the confidence of the beginner, than a plant
that fails to fulfil its expectations. Time, money and effort will be wasted if plants are
bought in haste.

■ Know what you want, and what to look for, and do not be tempted into making impulse buys. Note down the names of any plants that are unfamiliar to you and then study their needs at home before buying them.

■ Never buy from shops that display plants outside during the winter, or from market stalls. The plants are grown in warm, humid greenhouses and, however attractive they may look, very few will continue to flourish once they have been exposed to such extremes.

■ Similarly, do not be tempted by apparent bargains. It will be difficult to restore any plant that is already failing to full health. The size and type will always be reflected in the price. Large, slow-growing specimens will be much more expensive than rapidly grown annuals.

■ Check that plants are firmly rooted and in moist compost. Many garden centres display their plants on capillary matting, which normally indicates constant supplies of water. However, always check that the compost is not shrinking away from the sides of the pot, for if the pots have not been firmly pressed down on to the mat, the watering system will not have operated.

■ Fibrous roots will grow through the base of the pot when a capillary watering system is used, but discount any plants with larger roots showing. Pot-bound plants tend to be starved of food, therefore it is not a good idea to instantly pot-on newly acquired plants.

■ Leggy plants, with unnaturally widely-spaced foliage and pale leaves will have been under-exposed to light.

■ Avoid multi-stemmed plants with hollow-looking centres. Ensure shrubby plants are well branched and that bushy annuals are bushy.

■ Climbers should have several growing points. Ignore any tall-growing plants with broken leaders.

■ Ensure that the variegations on leaves are true and not merely blemishes. Avoid plants with plain leaves, unless it is a juvenile form.

■ Check carefully for brown leaf edges and tips.

■ Flowering plants should have plenty of buds just showing colour, and a few open flowers. This is particularly important if plants have been "forced" into flower out of their natural season. Flowers will fail to develop if they have been sold-on too quickly.

■ Look for any sign of pests and diseases, particularly eggs, on the undersides of leaves and at leaf junctions.

■ No plant is worth buying unless you are allowed to inspect it thoroughly. Always check a wrapped plant. Plants are sometimes offered for sale in sealed transparent bags, which, rather like Wardian cases, provide a complete micro-climate. Never break these seals; it is always possible to see exactly what you are buying through the wrapping. Never buy a plant if the seal has been broken.

■ Any plant bought during the winter should be well wrapped before it is taken outside. It is always better to buy tropical plants during their growing season.

■ Ensure that you can safely transport any plant before buying it. Stems and leaf tips are easily, and irreparably, damaged. Never leave plants in cars for long periods.

■ Consider the size of plant carefully. Large plants demand less patience and will be more robust than a plant of similar size grown at home, as long as you are sure you can provide ideal conditions. However, they will not be worth the extra cost if conditions are less than favourable. In these circumstances, it may be better to buy smaller plants and allow them to adjust to the available conditions, as they will then develop strong growth patterns.

ACCLIMATIZING BOUGHT PLANTS
■ Immediately place all winter-flowering plants in their final position, making sure that they have sufficient light.
■ All other plants should be placed in a warm room, out of draughts and away from bright light. Maintain a humid atmosphere, but only water if the compost is dry.
■ Monitor them carefully over a two week period to ensure that they are not suffering from pests and diseases; these will rapidly spread to other plants unless controlled at this stage.
■ Acclimatize plants, which are to be grown in cooler conditions, slowly. Water cautiously.
■ Feed the plants when you are sure that they have adjusted.

A-Z OF

THE PLANT DIRECTORY
Entries in the *Plant Directory*
are arranged alphabetically by
genus name. If you only know
the common name, consult
the index, which has both
common and Latin names.

The illustration contains
all the features of the *Plant
Directory* entries. Each feature
has been pointed out and
labelled to help you to make
full use of the information
given.

The *Care* and *Grower's
guide* sections contain all the
most important points of the
plant's care and maintenance,
such as watering, feeding,
potting-on, pruning, pests,
diseases, cleaning, and
display.

More detailed information
on plant care, pests and
diseases, and other problems
can be found on pp 140-4 and
150-3.

Details of foliage or flowers.

*There is always a silhouette of a
typical plant, which portrays its
form and average height.*

*Quick reference symbols
indicate the light, temperature
and humidity requirements of
each plant.*

*The plant is identified by its
Latin name, followed by its place
of origin and by its generally-
accepted common name.*

*Each entry begins with an
indication of the plant's height
and details of its light,
temperature and humidity
requirements.*

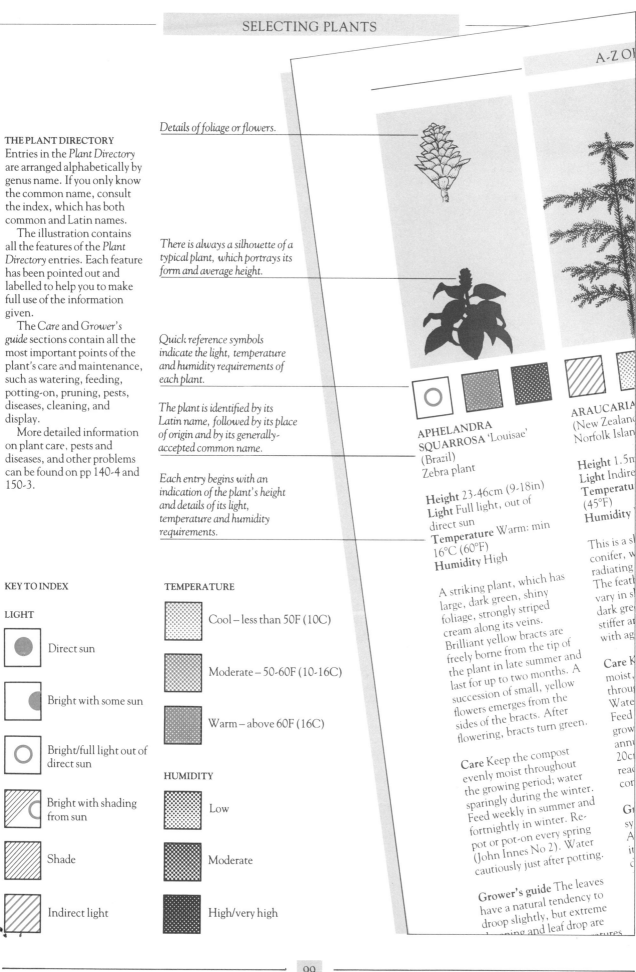

**APHELANDRA
SQUARROSA** 'Louisae'
(Brazil)
Zebra plant

Height 23-46cm (9-18in)
Light Full light, out of
direct sun
Temperature Warm: min
16°C (60°F)
Humidity High

A striking plant, which has
large, dark green, shiny
foliage, strongly striped
cream along its veins.
Brilliant yellow bracts are
freely borne from the tip of
the plant in late summer and
last for up to two months. A
succession of small, yellow
flowers emerges from the
sides of the bracts. After
flowering, bracts turn green.

Care Keep the compost
evenly moist throughout
the growing period; water
sparingly during the winter.
Feed weekly in summer and
fortnightly in winter. Re-
pot or pot-on every spring
(John Innes No 2). Water
cautiously just after potting.

Grower's guide The leaves
have a natural tendency to
droop slightly, but extreme

ARAUCARIA
(New Zealand
Norfolk Islan

Height 1.5m
Light Indire
**Temperatu
(45°F)
Humidity

This is a s
conifer, w
radiating
The feath
vary in s
dark gre
stiffer a
with ag

Care K
moist,
throu
Wate
Feed
grow
ann
20c
rea
co

**G
s
A
it

KEY TO INDEX

LIGHT

⬤ Direct sun

◑ Bright with some sun

○ Bright/full light out of
direct sun

▨ Bright with shading
from sun

▧ Shade

▧ Indirect light

TEMPERATURE

▦ Cool – less than 50F (10C)

▦ Moderate – 50-60F (10-16C)

▦ Warm – above 60F (16C)

HUMIDITY

▦ Low

▦ Moderate

▦ High/very high

ABUTILON STRIATUM
'Thompsonii'
(Brazil)
Flowering maple

Height 1.2m (4ft)
Light Full light, out of direct sun
Temperature Cool: min 7°C (45°F)
Humidity Moderate

A tall, free-flowering plant, which bears bell-shaped, orange flowers with crimson veins, either singly or in clusters, throughout spring and summer. Fine, maple-shaped leaves, mottled green and yellow, hang from its arching stems.

Care Water freely from spring to autumn, but keep the compost almost dry during the winter. Feed fortnightly during the growing season and pot-on annually in a well-drained, loam-based compost (John Innes No 2).

Grower's guide Provide support for the tall stems. Trim back side shoots during the summer and, after flowering, reduce the height of the main stems by half. Grow in a well-ventilated position. Prone to attack by mealy bug.

ACACIA ARMATA
(Australia)
Kangaroo thorn

Height 1m (3ft) or more
Light Bright, with some sun
Temperature Cool: min 5°C (40°F)
Humidity Dry

A shrubby plant, which provides welcome colour at the end of winter when the rich, yellow flower heads appear, either singly or in pairs, from amongst the dark green, spiny foliage. *Acacia armata* is an attractive plant for cooler areas.

Care Keep the compost evenly moist throughout the summer, but water sparingly during the winter. Give the plant a weekly liquid feed from bud formation until the end of flowering. Pot-on in the spring when necessary; normally every two to three years. Use a peat-based compost.

Grower's guide Prune back straggly growth after flowering. Grow in a well-ventilated position, with maximum light during the winter.

ACALYPHA HISPIDA
(Pacific Islands)
Chenille plant

Height 1.5m (5ft)
Light Full light, out of direct sun
Temperature Warm: min 16°C (60°F)
Humidity Very high

A striking plant, which demands consistently high levels of warmth and humidity. The 25-30cm (10-12in), bright crimson, catkin-like flower spikes appear in profusion during the summer, and sporadically throughout the rest of the year.

Care Keep the compost evenly moist at all times. Water less frequently during the winter. Feed weekly when the plant is growing actively. Examine the root ball regularly and pot-on whenever necessary, in a peat-based compost.

Grower's guide Cut back tall-growing plants in spring. Remove dying flower bracts promptly. Prone to attack by red spider mite and mealy bugs if its cultural requirements are not met. Keep away from direct sources of heat.

ACHIMENES
(Guatemala)
Hot water plant

Height 30cm (1ft)
Light Full light, out of direct sun
Temperature Warm: min 13°C (55°F)
Humidity High

This is a brightly coloured, free-flowering plant, with trailing stems and bright green, hairy leaves. Tubular flowers cover the plant from summer to late autumn, blooming in shades of pink, dark red and deepest mauve.

Care Keep the compost moist at all times during flowering. Feed monthly from bud formation until flowers begin to fade. The foliage will die back after flowering, but the rhizome may be dried out and re-started in spring.

Grower's guide Pinch out growing tips regularly to encourage a bushier habit. Avoid wetting hairy leaf surfaces and blooms when misting. Prone to attack by red spider mite in dry atmospheres.

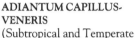

ADIANTUM CAPILLUS-VENERIS
(Subtropical and Temperate zones)
Maidenhair fern

Height 23cm (9in)
Light Shade
Temperature Warm: min 13°C (55°F)
Humidity Very high

A lovely fern, with light green fronds of small, fragile leaflets, which are held in an arching shape by dark, wiry stems.

Care Keep the compost moist at all times, but never allow it to become waterlogged. Reduce watering during winter. Feed fortnightly during the growing season. Pot-on when necessary in spring; mix some coarse sand with a peat-based compost to ensure good drainage.

Grower's guide Water-logging will result in immediate root rot. Increase humidity if fronds develop brown tips. The fine foliage will wilt if conditions are either too wet or too dry — check compost. Fronds will lose their colour if the light is too bright.

AECHMEA FASCIATA
(Brazil)
Urn plant

Height 60cm (2ft)
Light Full light, out of direct sun
Temperature Warm: min 16°C (60°F)
Humidity High

This large, dramatic bromeliad has stiff, silvery, grey-green, banded leaves, which form a funnel-shaped rosette with a central vase. The colourful pink bracts may emerge from the vase at any time of the year, and will last for up to four months. The foliage will begin to die off when flowering commences, but it will remain attractive for a considerable time.

Care Keep the central vase filled with water while the plant is growing. Use rainwater in hard water areas. Empty and re-fill vase every two to three months. Keep compost just moist throughout the year. Feed monthly — either through the vase or with a foliar spray.

Grower's guide Browning leaf tips — either increase watering or humidity. The plant will rot if the compost is too wet. Prone to attack by scale insects and mealy bug.

AGLAONEMA COMMUTATUM
(Philippines)
Chinese evergreen

Height 60cm (2ft)
Light Indirect
Temperature Moderate: min 13°C (55°F)
Humidity High

A. *commutatum* has large, spear-shaped leaves, which grow on long stems from a short, fleshy trunk. 'Silver Queen' has grey-green leaves with attractive silvery markings.

Care Water thoroughly during the growing period, but sparingly in winter. Feed monthly during the summer and pot-on, in a shallow pot, every three years. Use a peat-based compost.

Grower's guide Ensure constant temperatures and always avoid draughts. Shrivelled leaves and brown tips are caused by dry atmospheres. Prone to attack by red spider mite. Check frequently for mealy bug at the base of the leaf stalks.

ANTHURIUM SCHERZERIANUM
(Guatemala)
Flamingo flower

Height 37cm (15in)
Light Full light, out of direct sun
Temperature Warm: min 13°C (55°F)
Humidity Very high

An exotic-looking plant with large, waxy, red flower spathes, which have curious curly, orange tails growing from their centres. The flowering season extends over several months; each bloom lasting for several weeks. Long, dark green, spear-shaped leaves grow on slender stalks directly from the compost. Aerial roots grow around the base of the plant.

Care Water freely throughout the summer. Reduce watering during the winter, but never allow the root ball to dry out. Feed fortnightly during the growing season. Pot-on, or top-dress, annually. Fill one third of the pot with crocks, and pack sphagnum moss around the aerial shoots to encourage them to grow into the peat-based compost.

Grower's guide Ensure constant levels of heat and humidity. Prone to attack by aphids and red spider mite.

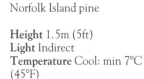

APHELANDRA SQUARROSA 'Louisae' (Brazil)
Zebra plant

Height 23-46cm (9-18in)
Light Full light, out of direct sun
Temperature Warm: min 16°C (60°F)
Humidity High

A striking plant, which has large, dark green, shiny foliage, strongly striped cream along its veins. Brilliant yellow bracts are freely borne from the tip of the plant in late summer and last for up to two months. A succession of small, yellow flowers emerges from the sides of the bracts. After flowering, bracts turn green.

Care Keep the compost evenly moist throughout the growing period; water sparingly during the winter. Feed weekly in summer and fortnightly in winter. Re-pot or pot-on every spring (John Innes No 2). Water cautiously just after potting.

Grower's guide The leaves have a natural tendency to droop slightly, but extreme drooping and leaf drop are the result of low temperatures or lack of water. Always give soft, tepid water. Leaf tips will brown in dry, hot air.

ARAUCARIA EXCELSA (New Zealand)
Norfolk Island pine

Height 1.5m (5ft)
Light Indirect
Temperature Cool: min 7°C (45°F)
Humidity Low

This is a slow-growing conifer, with tiered branches radiating from a central stem. The feathery-looking needles vary in shade from pale to dark green. They become stiffer and more prickly with age.

Care Keep compost evenly moist, but never waterlogged, throughout the summer. Water sparingly in winter. Feed monthly during the growing season and top-dress annually in spring once a 20cm (8in) pot size has been reached. Use a peat-based compost.

Grower's guide Encourage a symmetrical shape by growing A. excelsa alone and turning it regularly. It will tend to deteriorate over the height of 1.5m (5ft), so restrict growth by keeping the plant pot-bound. Lower leaves of mature plants will drop naturally, but leaf loss will also occur if compost is waterlogged or temperatures are too high.

ASPARAGUS PLUMOSUS (South Africa)
Asparagus fern

Height 1m (3ft)
Light Indirect
Temperature Moderate: min 7°C (45°F)
Humidity Moderate

These fast-growing members of the lily family have graceful, horizontal branchlets of very fine feathery foliage, which spring from upright slender stems. Mature plants may develop a climbing habit.

Care Water regularly during the growing season, but keep the compost just moist during the winter. Feed monthly during late spring and summer. Pot-on when necessary in spring. Use a loam-based compost, with some added sand to ensure good drainage.

Grower's guide Provide support for mature plants with climbing shoots. The shoots may be removed to retain the plant's bushy habit. Never allow the plant to stand in water. Red spider mite may cause the foliage to turn a dull bronze.

ASPARAGUS SPRENGERI (South Africa)

Height 1m (3ft)
Light Indirect
Temperature Moderate: min 7°C (45°F)
Humidity Moderate

This is a very suitable plant for hanging baskets — long, slender, arching stems cascade from its pot. Asparagus sprengeri is also ideal for training over trelliswork to create a lacy backdrop for other plants.

Care Keep the compost evenly moist, but never waterlogged, during the growing season. Water sparingly in winter. Feed monthly during spring and summer. Pot-on when the roots are filling the pot. Use a loam-based mixture (John Innes No 2), with some added sand.

Grower's guide Trim back in spring to encourage branching. Never allow the plant to stand in water. Leaves will yellow and drop in dry, hot conditions. Prone to attack by scale insects and red spider mite.

 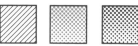 

ASPIDISTRA ELATIOR
(China)
Cast iron plant

Height 50cm (20in)
Light Shade
Temperature Cool: min 7°C (45°F)
Humidity Low

A handsome, large-leaved foliage plant, whose toughness is reflected in its common name. Long, lance-shaped, glossy, dark green leaves grow directly from the compost on stiff stalks. Small purple flowers may appear at the base of the plant.

Care Keep compost just moist during the summer and almost dry in winter. Feed monthly during the growing period. Pot-on in spring when pot-bound. Use a loam-based compost (John Innes No 2).

Grower's guide Clean leaves regularly with soft, tepid water. Never use leaf shine. Leaf tips will brown if exposed to direct sunlight. Plant collapse is normally due to overwatering or to waterlogged conditions.

ASPLENIUM BULBIFERUM
(Pacific Islands)
Spleenwort

Height 60cm (2ft)
Light Indirect
Temperature Warm: min 10°C (50°F)
Humidity High

Bushy shaped plants, with finely divided mid-green fronds, growing from wiry stems. Mature plants develop small plantlets on the upper surfaces of their fronds. These may be detached and grown on separately.

Care Keep the compost evenly moist at all times; reduce watering in winter. Never allow the plant to stand in water. Feed fortnightly from spring to autumn. Pot-on when the root ball is filling the pot. Use a peat-based compost, with added coarse sand for extra drainage. Take care not to bury the crown of the plant when re-potting.

Grower's guide Fronds will rapidly dry out in dry air. Prone to attack by scale insects.

ASPLENIUM NIDUS
(Tropical Asia)
Bird's nest fern

Height 60cm (2ft)
Light Indirect
Temperature Warm: min 13°C (55°F)
Humidity High

A rosette-forming fern, with undivided fronds, which flourishes in a shady corner. The bright green glossy foliage has slightly wavy margins and distinct, dark central ribs.

Care Keep the compost evenly moist throughout the year; reduce watering during the dormant period. Never allow the plant to stand in water. Feed fortnightly from spring to autumn. Potting-on may be necessary at any time of the year, whenever the root ball is filling the container. Use a peat-based compost, mixed with a little coarse sand or coarser peat.

Grower's guide Prone to attack by aphids and scale insects.

AZALEA INDICA
(India)
Azalea

Height up to 60cm (2ft)
Light Full light, out of direct sun
Temperature Cool: max 10°C (50°F)
Humidity Low

An attractive winter-flowering pot plant, which bears clusters of single or double blooms, in shades of pink, orange, red or white.

Care Water frequently to maximize the flowering period. A water mark, 12mm (½in) from the base of the stem, indicates that the correct amount is being given. Immerse the pot two or three times a week, but never allow it to stand in water. Never feed when in flower. Place outside after flowering and keep compost moist throughout the summer. Bring inside when new buds begin to form. Pot-on in peat-based compost.

Grower's guide Select plants with plenty of buds and a few open flowers. Remove faded blooms promptly. Water with rainwater in hard water areas. Yellowing leaves (chlorosis) are a symptom of lime conditions; water plant with sequestrated iron.

**BEAUCARNEA
RECURVATA**
(Mexico)
Pony-tail plant

Height 1.8m (6ft)
Light Bright, with some sun
Temperature Moderate: min
10°C (50°F)
Humidity Dry

An extraordinarily unusual-
looking plant, with a pony-
tail tuft of long, thin, strap-
like leaves, which grow from
the top of a tall woody stem.
The turnip-shaped base of the
stem stores water.

Care Water thoroughly, but
allow compost to almost dry
out before re-watering.
Feed monthly during the
growing season. Re-pot when
necessary, in spring. Use a
peat-based compost.

Grower's guide Peel off the
foliage as it fades. The plant
will tolerate occasional
dryness, but overwatering
will rot the swollen stem.

BEGONIA × 'Lucerna'
(Brazil)
Spotted angel's wing begonia

Height to 1.8m (6ft)
Light Full light, out of
direct sun
Temperature Moderate:
13°C (55°F)
Humidity Moderate

This is one of the fibrous-
rooted begonias, with tall
cane stems. The large olive
green leaves are silver-
flushed above and slightly
pink below. Clusters of pink
flowers are freely borne
through spring and summer.
Other cane-stemmed
varieties include *B. coccinea*,
which has glossy leaves with
red margins, and spotted
B. argenteo-guttata.

Care Water regularly during
the growing season, but allow
the compost to almost dry out
in between waterings. Keep
barely moist during the
winter. Feed every two weeks
during the summer. Pot-on,
when necessary, in a peat-
based compost.

Grower's guide Provide
plants with supports and tie
the stems in place at frequent
intervals. Cut back in spring
to encourage a bushy habit.
Avoid mildew by growing
plants in well-ventilated,
humid positions.

BEGONIA MASONIANA
(South East Asia)
Iron cross begonia

Height 25cm (10in)
Light Full light, out of
direct sun
Temperature Moderate: min
13°C (55°F)
Humidity Moderate

These are beautiful foliage
plants, with large, deeply
quilted, pale green, heart-
shaped leaves. The common
name refers to the distinctive
dark brown crosses, which
intersect the leaf centres.
Fine, velvety hairs entirely
cover the leaves and the
fleshy, pink stalks.

Care Water regularly during
the growing season, but allow
the compost to almost dry out
before re-watering. Keep just
moist in the winter. Feed
monthly during the summer.
Pot-on when necessary.
Allow the rhizome to rest just
on the surface of the peat-
based compost in a half-pot.

Grower's guide Avoid
wetting the rhizome when
watering. Cold damp
conditions will attract
mildew.

BEGONIA REX
(Assam)

Height to 30cm (1ft)
Light Full light, out of
direct sun
Temperature Moderate: min
13°C (55°F)
Humidity Moderate

This begonia is grown for
its dramatically-patterned
foliage. The large, heart-
shaped leaves are highly
coloured in shades of pink,
green, red and purple.

Care Water regularly during
the growing season, but allow
the compost to almost dry out
in between waterings. Keep
the compost barely moist
during the winter. Feed
every two weeks during
the summer. Pot-on when
necessary, in spring. Use
a peat-based compost and
wide, shallow containers.

Grower's guide Select plants
with well-shaped leaves and
no browning or curling edges.
Check carefully for fungal
disease. *B. rex* is particularly
prone to mildew; avoid cold,
damp, airless conditions. The
foliage is easily damaged —
never mist leaves directly.
Grow plant away from gas
fumes. A short-lived plant of
one to two years when grown
in ordinary room conditions.

BEGONIA SEMPERFLORENS
(Brazil)
Wax begonia

Height 15-23cm (6-9in)
Light Full light, out of direct sun
Temperature Moderate: min 10°C (50°F)
Humidity Low

These begonias are compact plants, with small, rounded, glossy-green or purple-red leaves. Masses of pink or white flowers are freely borne throughout the summer and, in the right conditions, will continue to appear to the end of autumn.

Care Keep well-watered during the growing season, but allow compost to almost dry out in between waterings. Keep barely moist during the winter. Feed monthly during the summer. Pot-on in spring when the roots are filling the pot. Use a peat-based compost.

Grower's guide Give maximum light during the winter; this will encourage good flowering and leaf colouration. Deadhead frequently to maintain attractive appearance.

BEGONIA × TUBERHYBRIDA
(South America)

Height to 60cm (2ft)
Light Full light, out of direct sun
Temperature Moderate: min 13°C (55°F)
Humidity Moderate

A group of tuberous hybrids, which flower in the summer. The Grandiflora group have bright double flowers up to 15cm (6in) in diameter. The petals may be frilled or margined in contrasting colours. The Multiflora varieties have numerous, small, single flowers, while the Multiflora Maxima group carry large sprays of double blooms.

Care Water regularly, but allow the compost to dry slightly between waterings. Feed every two weeks from early summer to when the flowers begin to die.

Grower's guide Support stems. Always mist around blooms. Overwatering will result in pale, rotting stems. Low humidity will result in bud drop, browning leaf tips, red spider mite and aphids. Foliage dies back at end of season.

BELOPERONE GUTTATA
(Mexico)
Shrimp plant

Height 46-60cm (1½-2ft)
Light Full light, out of direct sun
Temperature Moderate: min 7°C (45°F)
Humidity Moderate

The common name describes the small white flowers, with their overlapping, salmon-coloured bracts, which resemble a shrimp's body. The flowers hang on arching stems above pointed, oval leaves. They appear in early spring and are borne continuously for approximately nine months.

Care Keep compost thoroughly moist from spring to late autumn, but never allow the plant to stand in water, or to become waterlogged. Reduce watering in winter. Feed weekly during the summer. Pot-on, when necessary, in spring. Use a peat-based compost.

Grower's guide Remove the first flowers to encourage vigorous growth and maximum flowering period. Cut back stems by half at the end of the flowering season to promote bushy forms.

BILLBERGIA NUTANS
(South America)
Queen's tears

Height 46cm (18in)
Light Full light, out of direct sun
Temperature Moderate: min 7°C (45°F)
Humidity Low

An easily-grown bromeliad, with narrow, green, grass-like stems. Clusters of arching green and purple flower heads hang from pink bracts throughout the summer.

Care Keep vase filled with tepid water and the compost consistently moist throughout the growing and flowering season; during the winter, keep vase and compost just moist. Always use rainwater or softened tap water. Give monthly feeds during the summer and, where possible, stand plant outside to reinforce growth. When the rosette is too large for the pot, cut out old flowered rosettes and pot-on. Use a peat-based compost.

Grower's guide Avoid buying plants with open blooms and ensure that young plants are well-rooted. Brown leaf tips are the result of cold, dry air or cold water. If necessary, sink pots in containers of moistened peat.

BOUGAINVILLEA
(Brazil)

Height 2.4m (8ft)
Light Bright
Temperature Moderate: min 7°C (45°F)
Humidity Low

This flamboyant, summer-flowering climber is covered with an abundance of papery bracts in brilliant shades of purple, crimson, orange-red and golden yellow. The bracts last for several months, fading through a range of beautiful shades as they age.

Care Water freely during the growing period, but keep the compost almost dry after the leaves have dropped. Feed fortnightly throughout the summer. Pot-on young plants annually in a rich loam-based compost (John Innes No 3). Top-dress mature plants.

Grower's guide Bougainvillea's deciduous nature makes it best suited to the conservatory. Small plants may be brought inside to flower, but the next year's blooms will suffer. Prune in spring — shorten main stems by one-third and side shoots back to two or three buds. Train in new growth as it appears.

BROWALLIA SPECIOSA
(Colombia)
Bush violet

Height 23cm (9in)
Light Bright, with some sun
Temperature Cool: max 10°C (50°F)
Humidity Dry

These bushy, summer-flowering plants are often grown to bloom in succession throughout the year. Charming, lavender-blue, five-petalled flowers, with white centres, are borne in profusion on the fragile, branching stems.

Care Keep the compost moist at all times and feed fortnightly when growth is vigorous. Discard after flowering.

Grower's guide Pinch out growing tips regularly to encourage branching and good flowering. High temperatures will reduce the flowering period. Deadhead frequently to prevent plant setting seed. Prone to attack by aphids.

CALADIUM BICOLOR
'Candidum'
(Tropical South America)
Angel's wings

Height 30-46cm (1-1½ft)
Light Bright light, with shading from scorching sun
Temperature Warm: min 16°C (60°F)
Humidity Very high

Delicate, beautifully-hued, tuberous house plants, which die back to the crown in autumn. The huge, almost transparent, arrow-shaped leaves are white with delicate green and vivid red markings.

Care Water thoroughly throughout the summer, but never allow plant to sit in water. Ease up in autumn until the compost is almost dry. Feed weekly from spring until the leaves begin to fade. Provide maximum humidity by growing with other plants. Always protect from draughts.

Grower's guide Select plants with several stems rising from the crown. Store dormant tubers in pots, or boxes, of permanently moistened peat, in minimum winter temperatures. Pot-up in spring, ensuring a temperature of around 21°C (70°F). Gradually increase watering as shoots develop.

CALATHEA INSIGNIS
(Brazil)
Rattlesnake plant

Height 23cm (9in)
Light Full light, out of direct sun
Temperature Warm: min 13°C (55°F)
Humidity Very high

A densely-clustered foliage plant, with long, narrow, wavy-edged leaves, which grow on thin stems directly from the compost. The leaves are patterned alternately with emerald and dark green. The undersides are maroon-purple.

Care Water freely, with soft, tepid water, throughout the growing season. Water sparingly during the winter, but never allow the compost to dry out. Feed fortnightly from spring to late summer. Pot-on annually until a 20cm (8in) pot size is reached. Top-dress annually thereafter. Use a peat-based compost.

Grower's guide Cut off leaves as soon as they fade, or other parts of the plant may rot with them. Foliage will brown rapidly in dry atmospheres. Stems will rot in wet conditions. Prone to attack by red spider mite.

CALATHEA MAKOYANA
(Brazil)
Peacock plant

Height 60cm (2ft)
Light Full light, out of
direct sun
Temperature Warm: min
13°C (55°F)
Humidity Very high

Calatheas are a group of
particularly beautiful foliage
plants. *C. makoyana* has
leaves with pencilled bright
green veins, and dark green
blotches on a silver
background. The undersides
are a rich purple.

Care During the growing
season, water frequently with
soft, tepid water to maintain
an evenly moist compost.
Reduce watering in winter.
Feed weekly from spring to
autumn, and re-pot when
necessary in mid-summer.
Use a peat-based compost.

Grower's guide Do not buy
plants with browning leaf
tips. Calatheas require
consistently high levels of
humidity and warmth, which
makes them ideal plants for
bottle gardens or terrariums.
The leaves discolour in direct
sunlight. White deposits on
leaves are usually caused by
hard tap water.

CALLISTEMON CITRINUS
'Splendens'
(Australia)
Bottlebrush plant

Height 1.5m (5ft)
Light Full light, out of
direct sun
Temperature Cool: min 7°C
(45°F)
Humidity Dry

These make interesting
plants for the cool
conservatory. Shoots, with
narrow, tapering leaves are
adorned with bright red,
brush-like flower spikes in the
summer. *C. salignus* has vivid
yellow flower spikes.

Care Water freely throughout
the growing season,
whenever the compost begins
to dry out. Water sparingly
during the winter. Feed
fortnightly from spring to
early autumn. Pot-on in
spring. Use a loam-based
compost (John Innes No 3).
The large root systems will
need 25cm (10in) pots.

Grower's guide Prune the
stems in early spring.
Ventilate freely during warm
weather.

CAMELLIA JAPONICA
(China and Japan)

Height 1.5m (5ft)
Light Bright, shaded from
direct sun
Temperature Cool: min 7°C
(45°F)
Humidity Low

The large, single or double,
waxy blooms are set amongst
glossy, green foliage during
late winter and early spring.
The flowers are in shades of
pink, red or white and may be
plain or variegated.

Care Keep compost moist
at all times, but never
waterlogged. Use softened
water — camellias are lime-
haters and will not tolerate
alkaline conditions. Water
with sequestrated iron during
spring and summer. Pot-on,
when absolutely necessary, in
a peat-based compost. Plants
thrive when their roots are
constricted.

Grower's guide Yellowing
veins are due to chlorosis
and should be treated with
sequestrated iron. Never
move plant once buds have
formed and avoid draughts.
Lightly prune in late spring.
The cool winter conditions
demanded by camellias make
them ideal for the
conservatory or for other
winter-cool areas.

CAMPANULA ISOPHYLLA
(Italy)
Italian bell-flower

Trailing to 46cm (1½ft)
Light Full, out of direct sun
Temperature Cool: min 7°C
(45°F)
Humidity Low

A summer-flowering, trailing
plant, which has attractive,
grey-green, downy foliage.
Star-shaped flowers appear
in profusion throughout the
summer and may be blue,
white or lilac.

Care During the summer,
water thoroughly, but allow
the compost to dry slightly
before re-watering. Water
sparingly in winter. Feed
fortnightly throughout the
late spring and summer. Pot-
on annually in spring. Use a
peat-based compost.

Grower's guide Cut out any
straggly or unsightly shoots
when they appear and cut all
the growth down to compost
level after flowering. This
will ensure flowering along
the whole length of the stem
in the next year.

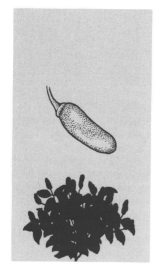

CAPSICUM ANNUUM
(Tropics)
Christmas pepper

Height 46cm (1½ft)
Light Bright, with some sun
Temperature Cool: max
13°C (55°F)
Humidity Moderate

Compact plants, with
brightly coloured fruits, or
'peppers', which emerge in
late summer, and remain on
the plant for several weeks.
The fruits may be rounded,
oblong, twisted, or conical in
shape and their colour will
ripen from green through
orange to red.

Care Water generously,
occasionally immersing pot to
the rim in a bowl of tepid
water, but allow the compost
to almost dry out in between
waterings, and never allow
the pot to stand in water.
Feed every 10 days from fruit
formation until they begin to
show colour. Discard plant
when fruits have dropped.

Grower's guide Select plants
with many green fruits and
grow in a well-ventilated
spot. Mist plant regularly
to discourage premature
dropping. Yellowing leaves
and red spider mite indicate
that the atmosphere is too
hot and dry.

CEROPEGIA WOODII
(Natal)
Rosary vine

Trailing to 1m (3ft)
Light Indirect
Temperature Moderate: min
10°C (50°F)
Humidity Low

A charming, trailing
succulent, which has dainty,
heart-shaped leaves, marbled
green and silver, growing in
pairs along wiry-thin, purple
stems. Clusters of small, pink
flowers appear in the autumn
and last up to six weeks.

Care During the summer,
water only when the compost
has nearly dried out, and
never allow the pot to stand
in water. Water very
sparingly in winter. Feed
monthly during the summer
and re-pot in the spring when
the pot is full of roots. Use a
rich loam-based compost
(John Innes No 2).

Grower's guide Choose
plants with several stems
and rich, green and white
leaves. Overwatering will rot
the stems. Yellowing leaves
indicate either overwatering
or low temperatures — check
compost immediately.
Remove tuber from wet soil
and allow it to dry out
slightly before re-potting.

CHAMAEDOREA ELEGANS
(Mexico)
Parlour palm

Height to 1.2m (4ft)
Light Indirect
Temperature Moderate: min
10°C (50°F)
Humidity Moderate

An ideal house plant, C.
elegans has upright, elegantly
arching branches and many
wide, grey-green leaflets.
Young plants may produce
small, green flowers, which
should be removed.

Care Water regularly during
the summer, but sparingly
during the dormant period.
Feed monthly during the
summer. Clean leaves by
sponging with tepid water.
Re-pot when the root ball
breaks through the surface
of the compost. Use a peat-
based compost and ensure
plant is firmed down well.

Grower's guide Brown spots
on leaves are usually the
result of overwatering or
the use of hard tap water.
Brown tips indicate lack of
humidity. Compost must be
free-draining; waterlogged
conditions cause root rot.
Prone to attack by red spider
mite and mealy bug if grown
in unsuitable conditions.

CHAMAEROPS HUMILIS
(Mediterranean)
European fan palm

Height 1.2m (4ft)
Light Full, out of direct sun
Temperature Warm: min
10°C (50°F)
Humidity Moderate

A statuesque plant, which
looks at its best when given
plenty of space to spread its
arching fronds. The leaflets
are arranged in stiff fans,
held out on long spiny stems.
Many new shoots will
develop in favourable
conditions.

Care Keep compost moist
through spring and summer,
but slightly drier during the
winter. Feed monthly during
the summer. Pot-on every
other year in a peat-based
compost.

Grower's guide Healthy tips
suddenly turning brown —
probably due to a drop in
temperature; but ensure that
plant is not exposed to
draughts or too near a direct
source of heat. Waterlogged
conditions will result in stem
and root rot. Prone to attack
by red spider mite in hot dry
atmospheres.

CHLOROPHYTUM COMOSUM 'Variegatum' (South Africa)
Spider plant

Height 1m (3ft) or more
Light Full light, out of direct sun
Temperature Moderate: min 7°C (45°F)
Humidity Low

Rosettes of grass-like, arching leaves, striped green and white, thrust up plantlets, which cascade on long shoots from the parent plant. Spider plants are always best grown in hanging baskets, with ample space for display.

Care Water liberally during spring and summer, but very sparingly in winter. In extremely hot, dry conditions, mist the plant frequently. Feed weekly during the summer and re-pot annually in spring. Use a peat-based compost.

Grower's guide Remove plantlets until the parent plant is well-formed. Increase watering if leaf tips begin to shrivel and turn yellow. Direct sources of heat will result in limp, pallid leaves. Browning leaf tips may indicate that plant needs re-potting, but might also be the result of dry air or lack of food.

CHRYSANTHEMUM (China and Japan)

Height 23-30cm (9-12in)
Light Indirect
Temperature Cool: max 10°C (50°F)
Humidity Low

These popular house plants are artificially dwarfed by growers and flowering is regulated by the controlled use of light, thus ensuring that plants will flower in succession throughout the year. Given the correct cultural conditions, blooms will last for up to eight weeks. Replace plant after flowering has finished.

Care Keep the compost permanently moist by watering thoroughly and regularly. Water more frequently in higher temperatures. Grow chrysanthemums on windowsills where they will just catch either early morning or evening light.

Grower's guide Only select plants with buds just showing colour, otherwise the buds may fail to open. Bud opening and flowering time will be accelerated in high temperatures, with a consequent reduction in length of flowering period. Underwatering will result in wilting and leaf fall.

CISSUS ANTARCTICA (Australia)
Kangaroo vine

Height up to 2.4m (8ft)
Light Indirect
Temperature Moderate: min 10°C (50°F)
Humidity Moderate

This fast-growing climber will cling to any support, quickly producing a curtain of shiny, oval leaves.

Care Water thoroughly from spring to autumn, but allow the compost to almost dry out before re-watering. Water sparingly in winter. Feed monthly during the summer. Re-pot annually in spring. Use a loam-based compost and line the pot with crocks.

Grower's guide Once a plant has started to cling, it will deteriorate rapidly if moved. Discourage growth by not potting-on beyond a 15cm (6in) sized pot and by only top-dressing annually. Browning foliage is normally due to lack of humidity; mist regularly in dry atmospheres. Overwatering will cause shrivelling, yellow or rotting leaves, mildew and root rot. Direct sunlight causes brown patches on leaves.

CISSUS DISCOLOR (East Indies)
Begonia vine

Height 2.4m (8ft)
Light Full, out of direct sun
Temperature Warm: min 16°C (60°F)
Humidity High

The upper surfaces of this decorative climber's leaves are embellished with bands of silver and green; the undersides are a rich purple.

Care A less tolerant plant than C. *antarctica*, it demands constantly warm, humid conditions. Water freely throughout the summer, but allow the compost to almost dry out before re-watering. Water sparingly in winter. Feed fortnightly during the growing period. Pot-on annually in spring until a 25cm (10in) pot size is reached, then top-dress. Use a free-draining loam-based mixture, with plenty of crocks around the base.

Grower's guide Some leaves will fall during the winter. Provide support for the stems and pinch out growing tips. Cut back main stem by one third in late winter to encourage new strong growth.

CITRUS MITIS
(Philippines)
Calamondin orange

Height 1m (3ft)
Light Bright, with some sun
Temperature Moderate, min 10°C (50°F)
Humidity Moderate

Citrus plants, with their strong fragrance and glossy-green foliage, make most attractive house plants, but most will not produce fruit until they are too large for the majority of households. The exception is C. mitis, which may flower and fruit when quite young. The fruits are excellent candied and make good marmalade.

Care Water thoroughly during the summer, whenever the surface feels dry. Keep compost just moist during the dormant period. Feed fortnightly during the flowering and fruiting period. Mist blooms frequently to encourage the fruit to set. Pot-on when necessary in a free-draining mixture of two parts loam and one part peat. Line a clay pot with crocks.

Grower's guide Place plant outside during the summer to ripen the wood — this will encourage fruiting and flowering. Clip into shape after fruiting.

CISSUS STRIATA
(Temperate regions)
Miniature grape ivy

Height 3m (10ft) or more
Light Full light, out of direct sun
Temperature Cool: min 7°C (45°F)
Humidity Low

A rampant, climbing or trailing plant, with delicate foliage which grows in profusion along fast-growing stems. The leaves, pink at first, mature to a dark green and are composed of five, tiny leaflets.

Care Water liberally during the growing season; sparingly in winter. Feed monthly during the summer. Pot-on in early spring. Use a peat-based mixture.

Grower's guide Pinch out growing tips to deter straggling habit. Provide support for climbing plants.

CLIANTHUS PUNICEUS
(New Zealand)
Parrot's bill

Height 3.5m (12ft)
Light Bright, with some sun
Temperature Moderate: min 5°C (40°F)
Humidity Dry

An attractive, summer-flowering climber, ideally suited to cultivation in a cool conservatory. Clusters of scarlet, pea-like flowers are borne from the bases of the fine, feathery leaves in late spring and early summer.

Care During the growing period, water thoroughly as soon as the compost begins to dry out. Reduce watering in winter. Feed monthly from bud formation until the end of the flowering period. Pot-on, or re-pot, annually in spring, using a peat-based compost.

Grower's guide Cut plants back after flowering. Train stems along canes or wires. Low winter temperatures are essential for early flowering; provide plenty of fresh air during the summer.
C. puniceus thrive in dry, hot atmospheres. Syringe in the early morning to discourage red spider mite.

CLIVIA MINIATA
(Natal)
Kaffir lily

Height 60cm (2ft)
Light Indirect
Temperature Cool: min 5°C (40°F)
Humidity Low

These flamboyant plants bear clusters of flame-coloured trumpets in spring and summer. When the flowering season has ended, C. miniata remains an attractive foliage plant, with almost evergreen, arching leaves.

Care Water moderately during the summer, allowing the compost to dry out slightly in between waterings. In winter give just sufficient water to prevent the compost from completely drying out. Feed monthly throughout the growing season. Cut off the flower head after blooms fade, but leave the stalk until it withers. Pot-bound plants flower most freely; only pot-on when the bulb is bursting out of the pot.

Grower's guide It is essential to rest plants in an unheated room over the winter. Never move the plant during bud formation or when in flower. Clivias grow best away from other plants.

CODIAEUM VARIEGATUM PICTUM
(Malaysia)
Joseph's coat

Height to 60cm (2ft)
Light Bright, with some sun
Temperature Warm: min 16°C (60°F)
Humidity Very high

This striking foliage plant demands very high humidity and consistent growing conditions. There are many exotic cultivars, with wide variations in leaf shape and colour.

Care During the growing season, water regularly and thoroughly with tepid water. Never allow the compost to dry out. Water sparingly in winter. Give weekly feeds during the summer. Pot-on annually in spring, using a loam-based compost. Clean leaves regularly by sponging with tepid water.

Grower's guide Fluctuating temperatures and draughts will result in instant leaf loss. Browning edges and tips of leaves are caused by low temperatures or dry air. Leaf colouring will dull if lighting levels are low. Red spider mite and scale insects will attack in poor conditions.

COFFEA ARABICA
(Ethiopia)
Coffee plant

Height 1.2m (4ft)
Light Indirect
Temperature Moderate: min 10°C (50°F)
Humidity Moderate

Although this attractive, shrub-like plant will not flower in the home, and therefore will not produce any beans, it is well worth growing just for its foliage. Its shiny dark green leaves have a slightly serrated edge.

Care Keep the compost evenly moist throughout the year, but increase watering during the growing period. Always give soft, tepid water. Use rainwater in hard water areas. Occasional misting of the leaves during the summer will keep them shiny and improve general humidity. Pot-on, when the roots are filling the pot — normally every two years. Use a peat-based compost. Pinch out the growing tips regularly to encourage bushy growth.

Grower's guide For a lower growing, more compact plant, prune back in spring.

COLEUS BLUMEI
(Java)
Flame nettle

Height 46cm (1½ft)
Light Full light, out of direct sun
Temperature Moderate: min 10°C (50°F)
Humidity Moderate

These bushy plants have brightly patterned, nettle-like foliage in shades of purple, red, bronze, yellow and green. Pinch out the flowers before they form in the summer. This will ensure a well-shaped plant.

Care Water regularly throughout the growing season to maintain an evenly moist compost. Pinch out the growing tips to encourage side shoots. Pot-on whenever necessary throughout the summer. C. blumei may be grown on to a good size over one season, but tend to become uncontrollably leggy. Plants are better discarded in the autumn.

Grower's guide Poor leaf colour is normally caused by over exposure to strong light, so provide shading from midday sun. Persistent leaf fall is normally due to lack of light.

COLUMNEA × BANKSII
(Costa Rica)
Goldfish plant

Trailing to 60cm (2ft)
Light Full light, out of direct sun
Temperature Moderate: min 13°C (55°F)
Humidity High

An exotic, winter-flowering trailer. The long stems are thickly clothed with small, glossy, mid-green, oval leaves. Hooded, scarlet flowers spurt from the stems on long thin stalks, appearing at any time from late autumn to spring.

Care Maintain the minimum temperature throughout the winter and keep the compost evenly moist. Increase watering during the summer. Feed weekly with diluted liquid fertilizer, and re-pot every two years in a peat-based compost.

Grower's guide Cut back stems after flowering. Mist leaves very frequently.

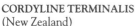

CORDYLINE TERMINALIS
(New Zealand)

Height 75cm (2½ft)
Light Indirect
Temperature Warm: min 13°C (55°F)
Humidity High

Oblong, pointed leaves spread out like a fan from its central stem. The lower leaves eventually drop, revealing a trunk topped with a foliage rosette. C. *terminalis* 'Firebrand' has glossy, mid-green leaves flushed red or purple. 'Tricolor' has distinct markings of creamy-white, pink and red.

Care The compost should be evenly moist throughout the year; reduce frequency of watering during the dormant period. Never allow the compost to become waterlogged. Give rainwater in hard water areas. Feed every ten days throughout the growing season. Pot-on in a peat-based compost when roots fill the pot.

Grower's guide Select plants with no trace of leaf browning or shrivelling. Brown leaf tips are normally due to uneven watering, but may also be caused by draughts or dry air. Leaves will curl in low temperatures.

CRYPTANTHUS ACAULIS
(South America)
Earth star

Height 8cm (3in)
Light Full light, out of direct sun
Temperature Warm: min 16°C (60°F)
Humidity Moderate

A decorative terrestrial-growing bromeliad, which is well-suited to terrariums, dish gardens and the lower branches of a bromeliad tree. The wavy leaves form a flattened ground-hugging rosette and, depending on the variety, are either mid-green, purple-brown or silver.

Care Water liberally during the growing season; sparingly in winter. Give occasional foliar feeds during the summer months. Potting-on is usually necessary, but small basal offsets can be detached in spring and potted-up separately. Use a peat-based mixture, with added leaf-mould or sphagnum moss.

Grower's guide Good light is essential to maintain leaf colour.

CTENANTHE
OPPENHEIMIANA 'Tricolor'
(Brazil)
Never-never plant

Height 30cm (1ft)
Light Indirect
Temperature Warm: min 18°C (65°F)
Humidity Very high

The narrow, pointed leaves of this compact plant are banded dark green and silver, with maroon undersides. C. *lubbersiana*, with dark green and yellow variegated leaves, is a slightly easier plant to care for; but, unfortunately, like the closely related marantas, all ctenanthe demand extremely high levels of humidity. Bottle gardens provide the ideal environment for them.

Care Keep compost constantly moist. Use soft, tepid water. Give a diluted liquid feed weekly during the summer. Pot-on every two years.

Grower's guide Low levels of humidity will result in dry, browning leaf tips and leaf drop. Move plants to a shadier position if the leaf edges roll up or become discoloured. Very prone to attack from red spider mite.

CYCAS REVOLUTA
(China)
Sago palm

Height 1.8m (6ft)
Light Bright, with some sun
Temperature Moderate: min 13°C (55°F)
Humidity Moderate

A rosette of spiny, feather-shaped, glossy-green fronds arch gracefully from the large trunk. C. *revoluta* is an extremely slow-growing palm, which produces only a few leaves annually, but given patience and a warm atmosphere, it does become a pleasing display plant.

Care Water thoroughly, but allow compost to almost dry out before re-watering. During the winter, water sparingly. Feed monthly during the summer. Potting-on will probably be necessary every two to three years. Use a loam-based compost.

Grower's guide Brown spots on leaves are due to overwatering or to cold water. Leaves will yellow if the plant is underwatered. Brown leaf tips are due to lack of humidity. Remove damaged leaves instantly — they will not recover and may damage the entire plant. Prone to attack by red spider mite in hot, dry conditions.

CYCLAMEN PERSICUM
(Mediterranean)

Height 46cm (1½ft)
Light Indirect
Temperature Cool: max
10°C (50°F)
Humidity Moderate

Red, pink, mauve or white
flowers, with attractive
swept-back petals, appear
in autumn and winter, and
are borne high above the
marbled-green foliage on
long slender stalks.

Care Keep compost moist,
but never waterlogged,
during the flowering season.
Never water the centre of the
plant, or mist the flowers and
foliage directly. Feed weekly
until plant is in bloom and
keep in a well-ventilated
position.

Grower's guide Select plants
with plenty of buds just
showing colour. After
flowering the foliage dies
back. Keep pot on its side in
a cool place until new shoots
appear in summer. Re-pot
corm and slowly move to a
warmer position. Subject to
botrytis and cyclamen mite.

CYPERUS ALTERNIFOLIUS
(Africa)
Umbrella plant

Height 75cm (2½ft) or more
Light Full light, out of
direct sun
Temperature Moderate: min
10°C (50°F)
Humidity High

Tall, rush-like stems carry
long, grass-like bracts on
their tips, which arch very
much like umbrella frames.
Green-yellow flower clusters
appear at the tops of the
stems in early summer.

Care Keep the compost
soaked throughout the year
by standing the pots in
containers filled with water.
These plants are moisture
lovers, and the roots should
never dry out. Feed once a
week throughout the year.
Pot-on annually in a loam-
based compost. Use John
Innes No 1 for young plants.

Grower's guide Remove
yellowing stems instantly to
encourage and provide space
for new growth. Browning
bract tips indicate lack of
humidity, or a pot-bound
plant.

CYRTOMIUM FALCATUM
(South East Asia)
Holly fern

Height 30-60cm (1-2ft)
Light Shade
Temperature Moderate: min
7°C (45°F)
Humidity Low

A tolerant fern with upright
fronds, which have pairs of
glossy, dark, holly-shaped
leaflets growing along their
entire length.

Care Keep the compost
evenly moist throughout the
year, but reduce frequency of
watering during the dormant
period. Feed fortnightly
during the summer. Potting-
on will probably be necessary
every other year — add some
leaf-mould to a peat-based
mixture.

Grower's guide High
temperatures and lack of
humidity result in yellowing
and browning of fronds and a
lack of new growth. Remove
dead and dying fronds
instantly, to provide space for
new growth. The light brown
spots, which form on the
underside of the fronds, are
the sporangia, or seeds.

DAVALLIA CANARIENSIS
(North Africa, Spain,
Canary Islands)
Hare's foot fern

Height 30-46cm (1-1½ft)
Light Full light, out of
direct sun
Temperature Moderate: min
7°C (45°F)
Humidity Low

A fern with arching deeply-
cut fronds, which are
displayed at their best
in hanging baskets. The
common name refers to the
furry rhizomes, which quickly
cover the surface of the
compost and overhang the
side of the pot.

Care Keep compost moist
throughout the year, but
water sparingly in winter.
Never allow the compost to
dry out. Give a fortnightly
feed throughout the summer.
Grow in a well-drained
compost; a mixture of equal
parts of sphagnum moss and
leaf-mould makes a good
anchorage for the roots.

Grower's guide Promptly
remove dead or damaged
fronds. Overwatering will
result in limp, yellow and
wilting fronds. In high
temperatures and/or dry air,
fronds will turn brown or
yellow and quickly die back.

DIEFFENBACHIA PICTA
(South America)
Dumb cane

Height to 1m (3ft)
Light Indirect
Temperature Warm: min
16°C (60°F)
Humidity High

A group of plants with
dramatically variegated
foliage. The large, oval leaves
are held upwards on long,
fleshy stems. *D. picta*
'Exotica' has deep green,
white-blotched leaves, which
are heavily suffused with
yellow. 'Rudolph Roehrs' has
pale, creamy-yellow leaves
and ivory veins. The sap from
the stems is poisonous.

Care Water regularly and
thoroughly during the
summer, allowing the
compost to dry out slightly
before re-watering. Water
sparingly in winter. Feed
fortnightly during the
growing season and re-pot in
spring. Use a rich compost
(John Innes No 3).

Grower's guide Allow plenty
of space for plant to grow
unimpeded. Overwatering
will result in stem rot.
Increase warmth and
humidity if the foliage begins
to wilt, turn yellow or drops.
Mature plants naturally lose
their lower leaves.

**DIZYGOTHECA
ELEGANTISSIMA**
(Australasia)
False aralia

Height 1.2m (4ft)
Light Full light, out of
direct sun
Temperature Warm: min
16°C (60°F)
Humidity Very high

An elegant, delicately-leaved
plant, with finger-like
serrated leaflets, which arch
gracefully from a central
stem. The foliage matures,
through copper and dark
green, to almost black.

Care Keep compost evenly
moist at all times, but water
carefully. Never allow the
root ball to dry out; but
reduce watering during the
winter. Feed fortnightly
during the growing season.
Pot-on, when necessary, in
a loam-based compost (John
Innes No 3).

Grower's guide Mature
plants lose their fine filigree
foliage — pinch out growing
tip during the dormant period
to retain juvenile growth.
Maintain a very humid
atmosphere to prevent leaf
drop.

DRACAENA DEREMENSIS
(Tropical Africa)
Striped dracaena

Height 1.2m (4ft)
Light Indirect
Temperature Moderate: min
13°C (55°F)
Humidity Moderate

Long, green and white-
striped, arching leaves rise
directly from the central
stem. In maturity, *D.
deremensis* has a tendency to
shed its lower leaves and is
best 'stopped' at 1.2m (4ft)
before it becomes too
ungainly.

Care Keep compost
thoroughly moistened,
but never waterlogged,
throughout the summer.
Water sparingly in winter.
Feed fortnightly during the
summer. Pot-on every two
years using a rich loam-based
compost with added peat.
Top-dress once a 15-17cm
(6-7in) pot size has been
reached.

Grower's guide Avoid
wetting the stem when
watering — direct contact
with wet or waterlogged soil
induces premature leaf fall;
similarly overwatering will
hasten loss of lower leaves.
Prone to attack by mealy bug.

DRACAENA FRAGRANS
(Tropical Africa)
Corn palm

Height 1m (3ft) or more
Light Full light, out of
direct sun
Temperature Moderate: min
13°C (55°F)
Humidity Moderate

A broad-leafed dracaena,
with an arching, almost
curling, habit. 'Massangeana'
has dark green leaves with
a broad, golden centre.
'Lindenii' has golden edges to
its gold and green leaves.

Care Keep the soil moist by
frequent watering from spring
to autumn; for the rest of the
year, water only when the
surface is dry. Feed
fortnightly during the
growing season. Pot-on,
when roots fill the pot;
normally annually for young
plants. Use a rich, loam-
based compost (John Innes
No 3).

Grower's guide *D. fragrans*
seems to grow particularly
well in group planting
schemes. Ensure sufficient
light for the leaf variegation
and check constantly for
mealy bug.

DRACAENA GODSEFFIANA 'Florida Beauty'
(Central Africa)
Gold dust dracaena

Height 60cm (2ft)
Light Bright, with some sun
Temperature Moderate: min 10°C (50°F)
Humidity Low

D. godseffiana has a very different form from the other dracaenas. It is a compact, shrubby plant, with oval-shaped, dark green leaves, which are heavily flecked with yellow.

Care Keep compost moist, but never waterlogged, during the summer. Reduce watering for the rest of the year, giving just enough to prevent the compost from completely drying out. Feed fortnightly during the growing period. Pot-on every other year. Use a rich, loam-based compost (John Innes No 3).

Grower's guide Leaf colouring will fade in low lighting levels. Stunted growth is normally due to attack from mealy bugs.

DRACAENA MARGINATA
(Tropical Africa)

Height 1.5m (5ft) or more
Light Full light, out of direct sun
Temperature Moderate: min 10°C (50°F)
Humidity Moderate

The easiest and toughest of the dracaenas. The long, fine, red-margined leaves fan out from the narrow central stem. The 'Tricolor' cultivar has fine green, cream and pink stripes, but is slightly more demanding.

Care Compost must be kept moist, but never waterlogged, throughout the summer. Water sparingly during the dormant period. Feed monthly during the summer. Potting-on will normally be necessary every other year. Use a rich, loam-based compost (John Innes No 3) and firm plant in well.

Grower's guide Cold damp conditions and waterlogged compost will result in yellowing leaves and premature leaf drop. Leaves will lose their fine colours in low lighting levels. Prone to attack by mealy bugs.

DRACAENA SANDERIANA
(Zaire)
Ribbon plant

Height 46cm (1½ft) or more
Light Indirect
Temperature Moderate: min 10°C (50°F)
Humidity Moderate

A compact, tolerant dracaena, bearing dense, ribbon-like foliage evenly up the central stem. The grey-green leaves have silver, wavy margins and, at 20cm (8in), are comparatively short.

Care Keep compost evenly moist from early spring to winter, but increase watering during the summer. During the dormant period, compost should be almost dry. Feed fortnightly through the summer and pot-on annually if a tall plant is required. *D. sanderiana* will grow to a height of 1.8m (6ft), but growth may be restricted by top-dressing compost, once a 13cm (5in) pot size has been reached. Use a rich, loam-based compost (John Innes No 3).

Grower's guide Do not leave plants on a cold windowsill on cold nights. Prone to attack by mealy bug.

EPIPHYLLUM
(Central and South America)
Orchid cactus

Height 60-90cm (2-3ft)
Light Full light, out of direct sun
Temperature Moderate: min 13°C (55°F)
Humidity Moderate

An epiphytic, forest cactus with two distinct flowering periods — late spring and autumn. Large, bell-shaped flowers emerge from the edges of two-year-old pads. They may be red (*Ackermannii* hybrids) or snow-white and yellow (*E. cooperi*).

Care Keep compost consistently moist when the plant is in flower and new pads are developing. Reduce watering slightly during the autumn; allow compost to almost dry out in the winter until the new flower buds begin to form. Give a high potassium fertilizer liquid feed, from bud development until the autumn flowering period is over. Re-pot annually, in early spring. Use a loam-based potting compost (John Innes No 2).

Grower's guide Provide support for the long stems. Never move plants once buds have formed. Ensure a cool winter resting period.

EPISCIA DIANTHIFLORA
(Mexico)
Lace flower vine

Spread 30cm (1ft) or more
Light Full light, out of
direct sun
Temperature Warm: min
13°C (55°F)
Humidity High

A very attractive trailing
plant, which is closely related
to the saintpaulia. The mid-
green, downy leaves grow in
clusters along fine purple
stems. Simple-petalled,
white, fringed flowers appear
in succession throughout the
summer.

Care Keep compost moist,
but never waterlogged,
throughout the summer;
reduce watering in winter.
Feed monthly from bud
formation to the end of
flowering. Pot-on, when
necessary, in a peat-based
compost.

Grower's guide E. dianthiflora
is best displayed in a hanging
basket, where the runners
will trail over attractively.
Shorten stems after
flowering; the small plantlets
will readily root to form new
plants. Mist plant frequently
in hot atmospheres.

**EUPHORBIA
PULCHERRIMA**
(Mexico)
Poinsettia

Height 30-46cm (1-1½ft)
Light Bright, with some sun
Temperature Warm: min
10°C (50°F)
Humidity Moderate

A popular winter-flowering
plant, with broad, bright
green leaves. The flowers are
greenish-yellow, small and
insignificant, but they are
surrounded by colourful
bracts. The bracts may be
pink or green, but are
normally red.

Care Water thoroughly, but
allow compost to almost dry
out before re-watering. The
leaves will droop slightly
when more water is required.
Keep well away from draughts
and fumes and avoid wild
fluctuations of temperature.
Discard plant after flowering.

Grower's guide Select plants
with fresh bracts: they will
have small intact flowers
in the centre. Insufficient
humidity will be indicated by
browning leaf edges and loss
of flower heads. The sap is
poisonous.

× FATSHEDERA LIZEI
(Garden hybrid)
Ivy tree

Height 1.8m (6ft) or more
Light Shade
Temperature Cool: min 2°C
(35°F)
Humidity Low

A cross between two separate
genera, Fatsia japonica and
Hedera helix, × Fatshedera
lizei is a strong climber, with
shiny, deeply-lobed leaves. It
will also form a bushy display
plant, provided the growing
tip is pinched out constantly.

Care Keep compost moist
throughout growing season;
water sparingly in winter.
Never allow compost to dry
out. Feed fortnightly during
the summer. Re-pot annually
in spring. Use a peat-based
compost.

Grower's guide Select plants
with healthy growing tip and
good dark colour. Provide
support for climbers. Pinch
out growing tips annually
to encourage side shoots.
Overwatering will result in
browning leaf edges. Lower
leaves will drop in hot,
dry atmospheres. Avoid
draughts. Prone to attack
by red spider mite.

FATSIA JAPONICA
(Japan)
Castor oil plant

Height 1m (3ft) or more
Light Indirect
Temperature Cool: min 7°C
(45°F)
Humidity Low

An upright, branching plant,
with large, glossy, lobed
leaves. It is a tolerant plant,
well-suited to cool airy
conditions, but also thriving
in warm rooms.

Care Water thoroughly,
from spring to autumn; but
sparingly during the winter.
Feed every two weeks during
the summer. Pot-on annually
in spring, using a loam-based
compost (John Innes No 2).
Mature plants will need 25cm
(10in) tubs.

Grower's guide If young
plants show no signs of
natural branching, pinch out
growing tips in the spring.
Clean leaves by occasionally
sponging with soft, tepid
water. Pale, spotted leaves
with dry edges indicate
underwatering. Mature plants
demand copious watering
during hot weather. Yellow,
drooping leaves indicate
overwatering. Foliage will
shrivel if exposed to direct
sun and/or dry air.

FICUS BENJAMINA
(India)
Weeping fig

Height 1-2m (3-6ft) or more
Light Full light, out of direct sun
Temperature Moderate: min 13°C (55°F)
Humidity Moderate

Elegant trees, with slender stems and gracefully arching branches, which bear glossy, mid-green, slender leaves.

Care Keep compost moist throughout the summer, but allow it to dry out slightly in between waterings. Water sparingly during the winter. Use tepid rainwater in hard water areas. Feed every two weeks during the growing season. Pot-on every two years. A peat-based compost, mixed with a little sand, will provide a well-drained medium.

Grower's guide *F. benjamina* will adapt to many different conditions, but once adapted resents any further change. Move plants only when absolutely necessary. Provide support for taller specimens. Brown and yellow patches, followed by leaf drop, are due to persistent draughts, dry air or overwatering. Check frequently for red spider mite and mealy bug.

FICUS ELASTICA
(Tropical Asia)
Rubber plant

Height 2.4m (8ft)
Light Full light, out of direct sun
Temperature Moderate: min 13°C (55°F)
Humidity Low

F. elastica 'Robusta' is the most well-known of these large, leathery-looking, oval-leaved plants; but other cultivars include 'Black Prince', with almost black leaves and the variegated 'Tricolor' and 'Doescheri'.

Care Water thoroughly during the growing season, but allow the compost to dry out slightly before re-watering. Water sparingly in winter. Avoid using hard tap water. Give fortnightly liquid feeds during the summer. Pot-on, when absolutely necessary, in spring.

Grower's guide Select plants with healthy growing tips. Brown and yellow patches, followed by leaf drop, are due to dry air. Prone to attack by red spider mite and mealy bug. Sponge leaves regularly with soft, tepid water. Encourage side shoots by removing the growing tip, once the plant has reached a height of 1.8m (6ft).

FICUS LYRATA
(West Africa)
Fiddle leaf fig

Height 1.2m (4ft)
Light Indirect
Temperature Warm: min 16°C (60°F)
Humidity Moderate

A single-stemmed ficus, with magnificent, waxy, wavy-edged leaves, which grow up to 46cm (18in) long. They are normally a mid-green, but may occasionally have yellow markings.

Care Water thoroughly throughout the growing season, but avoid waterlogging. Reduce watering during the winter. Give soft, tepid water. Feed every 10-14 days during the summer. Pot-on, in a peat-based compost, when absolutely necessary; the leggy habit of the plant will be deterred if root growth is restricted.

Grower's guide The removal of the growing tip may produce side shoots. A well-ventilated position during the summer will reduce the likelihood of leaf fall — normally due to lack of humidity, but also caused by underwatering or by direct sunlight. Maintain minimum temperature in the winter.

FICUS PUMILA
(China)
Creeping fig

Height 60cm (2ft) or more
Light Shade
Temperature Moderate: min 7°C (45°F)
Humidity High

A climbing or trailing plant, with thin, wiry stems and tiny, bright green, heart-shaped leaves, it provides ideal ground cover for taller-growing specimens.

Care Keep the compost evenly moist throughout the year; never allow it to dry out. The paper-thin leaves do not retain moisture in the way that fleshier leaves can. Re-pot when necessary; normally every two years. Use a peat-based compost.

Grower's guide Encourage the development of a spreading habit by frequently pinching out the growing tips of young plants. *F. pumila* will benefit from the joint humidity when grown among other plants; extra care should be taken to ensure that humidity levels are sufficiently high when plants are grown alone. Prone to attack by red spider mite and mealy bug.

FICUS RADICANS
'Variegata'
(East Indies)

Spread to 46cm (1½ft)
Light Full light, out of
direct sun
Temperature Moderate: min
13°C (55°F)
Humidity High

A strongly-variegated,
trailing plant. Its green and
white, pointed leaves have
slightly wavy, cream-white
edges. It will trail attractively
around other plants or look
equally effective growing by
itself in a hanging basket.

Care Keep the compost moist
from spring to autumn; the
root ball should never dry
out. In winter let the
compost dry slightly before
watering. Feed fortnightly
throughout spring and
summer. Pot-on annually
in spring. Use a peat-based
compost. Mature plants
should be top-dressed.

Grower's guide Encourage
naturally branching habit by
pinching out the growing tips
of young plants. Brown and
yellow patches, followed by
leaf drop, are due to dry air,
persistent draughts or
overwatering. Prone to attack
by scale insects. Mealy bugs
may cause leaf drop.

FITTONIA
ARGYRONEURA 'Nana'
(Peru)
Snakeskin plant

Spread 15cm (6in) or more
Light Shade
Temperature Warm: min
16°C (60°F)
Humidity Very high

A dense, low-growing creeper
with tiny, dark green leaves,
which have a beautiful
pattern of white veins. If
given sufficient humidity, it
will tolerate room conditions,
but thrives in bottle gardens.

Care Water thoroughly with
soft, tepid water during the
growing season. Keep
compost moist, but never
waterlogged. Water
cautiously during the
dormant period. Maintain
constantly warm temperature
and avoid draughts. Feed
monthly during summer. Re-
pot in spring, using a peat-
based compost.

Grower's guide Leaves
will yellow and wilt in
waterlogged conditions.
Remove plant from compost,
allow roots to dry for two
days and re-pot. Shrivelling
leaves indicate insufficient
humidity. Prone to attack by
red spider mite.

FUCHSIA
(Central and South America,
New Zealand)

Height Varies
Light Full, out of direct sun
Temperature Cool: min 7°C
(45°F)
Humidity Low

There are hundreds of named
varieties. Heights depend on
whether the plant is bush-
shaped, trailing or standard.
Pendulous, bell-shaped
flowers, in contrasting shades
of deep purple, pink, cream
and white, appear in early
summer and bloom until late
autumn.

Care Water freely during
the summer; keep compost
almost dry after leaf drop.
Feed weekly from spring to
autumn. Pot-on, or top-dress,
plants every spring. Use a
loam-based compost (John
Innes No 3).

Grower's guide Cut the
stems of bush and trailing
forms right down in spring.
Cut standards back to the
main stem. Do not pinch out
tips before the flowering
season. Leaf spot disease is
encouraged by overwatering
in winter. Prone to attack
by red spider mite in dry
atmosphere.

GARDENIA JASMINOIDES
'Florida'
(China)

Height to 1m (3ft)
Light Full light, out of
direct sun
Temperature Warm: min
10°C (50°F)
Humidity High

A shapely plant with dark
glossy leaves and fragrant
double white blooms, which
are borne in the summer.
Some varieties are winter-
flowering. Give consistently
warm daytime temperatures
during the growing period.
After flowering keep in
moderate temperatures.

Care Water well throughout
growing season; decrease in
the dormant period. Use
rainwater in hard water areas;
lime will turn leaves yellow.
Feed monthly in growing
season and fortnightly as buds
appear. Pot-on in spring,
using a peat-based compost.

Grower's guide After
flowering, cut back all shoots
by one half to two-thirds. If
plants have yellowing leaves,
treat with sequestrated iron.
Low levels of humidity may
lead to bud drop and
infestation by red spider mite.

GREVILLEA ROBUSTA
(New South Wales)
Silk oak

Height 1m (3ft) or more
Light Full light, out of
direct sun
Temperature Cool: min 7°C
(45°F)
Humidity Low

A small tree, with attractive,
fern-like, silky leaves, which
retain their mid-green,
juvenile colour until the
plant reaches a height of 1m
(3ft). Unfortunately, as the
plant matures, the leaf colour
changes to a dull, dark green
and the plant's interest is
lost.

Care Water thoroughly in
summer, sparingly in winter.
Never allow the root ball to
dry out. Grevilleas are lime-
haters and should always be
watered with rainwater in
hard water areas. Feed
fortnightly during the
summer. Pot-on annually in
spring, using a peat-based
compost.

Grower's guide Yellowing
leaves are most likely to be
caused by chlorosis; treat
with sequestrated iron.
Remove leaves as they turn
brown. Grevilleas thrive in
cool airy environments and
will benefit from a spell
outside during the summer.

GYNURA SARMENTOSA
(India)
Velvet plant

Height 60cm (2ft)
Light Full light, out of
direct sun
Temperature Moderate: min
13°C (55°F)
Humidity Dry

A richly-coloured plant, its
stems and dark green foliage
are covered with iridescent
purple hairs. Small flowers
appear in the spring, but their
smell is so unpleasant that it
is better to remove them.

Care Keep compost moist
throughout the growing
season, but water sparingly
during the winter. Mist
around the plant in very hot
or dry conditions, but avoid
wetting the leaves as they
are easily damaged. Feed
fortnightly during the
summer. Re-pot when
necessary in spring, using
a peat-based compost.

Grower's guide Pinch out
growing tips regularly to
encourage bushy growth. Cut
out straggly growth in spring.
Plants may be trained on
canes. After two to three
years the growth becomes
uncontrollable and the plant
is better discarded.

HEDERA
(Europe and Canary Islands)
Ivy

Height 1m (3ft) or more
Light Shade
Temperature Moderate: min
7°C (45°F)
Humidity Moderate

H. helix has many named
varieties. 'Little Eva' is plain
green with a cream margin.
'Little Diamond' and 'Adam'
have attractive grey and
white variegations. The
much larger-leafed,
H. canariensis 'Variegata'
has bold, green and white
markings and makes a tall-
growing climber, but does
need to be supported.

Care Keep compost moist
throughout the growing
season, but water sparingly in
winter. Never allow compost
to dry out. Avoid warm, dry
conditions and provide good
ventilation during the
summer. Feed monthly
during the summer. Pot-on in
a peat-based compost, when
the roots fill the pot.

Grower's guide The leaves
will lose their variegation if
the light is insufficient, or
if the plant is pot-bound.
Always remove plain leaves
to prevent the plant from
entirely reverting. Prune
plants in spring.

HELXINE SOLEIROLII
(Corsica)
Mind your own business

Height Prostrate
Light Full light, out of
direct sun
Temperature Moderate: min
7°C (45°F)
Humidity Low

An easily-cultivated,
prostrate creeper, which
forms mounds of minute, pale
green leaves. An attractive
ground cover plant, it also
forms a beautiful hummock
shape when grown alone.

Care Water freely in summer,
but more cautiously during
the winter. Pot-on in spring
when growing it as a separate
plant. Use a loam-based
compost (John Innes No 2).

Grower's guide Stem and
root rot will result from
overwatering. Underwatering
will result in the entire
plant rapidly turning brown.
The invasive habit of
H. soleirolii should be checked
occasionally, as it will readily
cover other low-growing
plants.

HEMIGRAPHIS COLORATA
(Malaysia)
Red ivy

Height Trailing
Light Bright, with some sun
Temperature Warm: min 13°C (55°F)
Humidity High

These brightly-coloured plants look their best in hanging baskets. In a good light the leaves are a bright, metallic-purple above, with reddish-purple undersides. In lower lighting levels they tend to develop a silvery colouring. Small white flowers may appear during the summer.

Care Water liberally throughout the growing season. In winter keep the compost just moist. Feed fortnightly from late spring to autumn. Pot-on, or top-dress, annually in a peat-based mixture.

Grower's guide Cut back straggling stems in early spring. Ensure adequate levels of warmth and humidity throughout the year.

HEPTAPLEURUM ARBORICOLA
(Australasia)
Parasol plant

Height 60-90cm (2-3ft)
Light Full light, out of direct sun
Temperature Warm: min 10°C (50°F)
Humidity Low

An elegant, densely-foliated display plant. Groups of shiny, dark green leaflets radiate from the tips of long, leafstalks, giving the plant its popular name.

Care Keep the compost evenly moist throughout the year; decreasing amount of water slightly during the dormant period. Feed monthly during the summer. Sponge leaves occasionally with cotton wool and tepid water. Pot-on when necessary, using a peat-based compost.

Grower's guide Avoid drastic leaf fall by maintaining constant temperatures. Blackened leaf tips are due to overwatering. Pinch out to shape when necessary, but do not remove the growing tip unless a lower shrubbier plant is required.

HIBISCUS ROSA-SINENSIS
(Asia)
Rose mallow

Height 1.8m (6ft)
Light Bright, shade from intense sun
Temperature Moderate: min 13°C (55°F)
Humidity Low

These handsome, shrubby evergreens have downy, heart-shaped leaves and lily-like blooms with prominent anthers. Flowers may be scarlet, yellow, orange, pink or white, and will appear almost continuously through the autumn.

Care Maintain an evenly moist compost throughout the summer; water sparingly in winter. Feed fortnightly during the growing season. Re-pot, or pot-on, annually in spring. Use a rich, loam-based compost.

Grower's guide Grow in a well-ventilated position — conservatories are ideal. Cut back to within 8cm (3in) of the old growth, at a strong bud, in early spring. Pinch out all new side shoots when they are 15cm (6in) long. Leaf curl indicates dry air. Prone to attack by aphids and red spider mite.

HIPPEASTRUM
(South America)

Height 75cm (2½ft)
Light Full light, out of direct sun
Temperature Warm: min 13°C (55°F)
Humidity High

Several large, trumpet-shaped blooms, in colours ranging from white to deepest red, are carried on tall, fleshy stems. Hippeastrum, frequently sold as amaryllis, naturally flower in spring or early summer, but specially prepared bulbs are available for winter flowering.

Care Bring potted bulbs into flower by placing them on a warm shelf. Water carefully. Increase watering as the buds appear. Move to a good light for flowering. Flowering length is maximized by cool conditions and cautious watering.

Grower's guide Remove flower stalk after flowering and feed fortnightly, until late summer, when bulb should be rested. Allow compost to dry out and once leaves have died back, place in a frost-free position until the new growth appears. Pot-on bulbs every two years in John Innes No 2.

HOWEA FORSTERIANA
(Lord Howe Island, South
Pacific)
Kentia palm

Height 3m (10ft)
Light Indirect
Temperature Warm: min
13°C (55°F)
Humidity Moderate

A slow-growing tolerant
palm, which makes an
elegant display plant. Fans
of pointed leaflets arch
gracefully from its upright
stems.

Care Water thoroughly,
throughout the growing
season; sparingly in winter.
Use soft, tepid water and
ensure good drainage. Never
allow pot to sit in water. Feed
monthly during the summer.
Pot-on in spring when the
root ball is pushing above the
surface. Top-dress annually
after a 20-25cm (8-10in) pot
size has been reached. Add a
little sand to a peat-based
compost and line the pot
with crocks.

Grower's guide Lower fronds
will die back naturally.
Underwatering, or dry air will
result in brown tips. Brown
spots on leaves are due to
overwatering or to hard tap
water. Prone to attack by red
spider mite.

HOYA BELLA
(India)

Height 23-30cm (9-12in)
Light Full light, out of
direct sun
Temperature Warm: 16°C
(60°F)
Humidity High

A small, spreading plant,
with twiggy, pendulous
branches, which is ideal for a
hanging container. Its pale
green leaves are often silver-
spotted. Trusses of heavily-
scented, waxy, white or pink
flowers are freely borne
throughout the summer.

Care Water frequently during
the growing and flowering
seasons, but sparingly in
winter. Allow the compost
to almost dry out in between
waterings. Feed every two to
three weeks throughout the
summer. Pot-on, when
necessary, in a peat-based
compost.

Grower's guide Never
remove the woody flower
stalks, as subsequent blooms
will appear from the same
point. Do not move plant
once the flower buds have
formed. Leaves will turn
brown if the plant is
overwatered.

HOYA CARNOSA
(Queensland)
Wax plant

Height 5m (16ft)
Light Full light, out of
direct sun
Temperature Moderate:
10°C (50°F)
Humidity Moderate

A vigorous climber, with
clinging aerial roots and
clusters of fragrant, white,
star-shaped flowers, which
hang from short stems. An
entire new length of stem
develops before any leaves
appear, and should be tied
in with the others around a
sphagnum moss-stick, or
trained up a trellis.

Care Water thoroughly
throughout the summer, but
sparingly in winter. Increase
temperature to 18°C (65°F)
as flower buds open. Feed
every three weeks during
the summer. Pot-on when
the plant is pot-bound,
in a peat-based compost.

Grower's guide Never move
the plant once the flower
buds have formed, and do not
remove the flower stalks.
Encourage branching from
the base by pinching out the
growing tips of young plants.
Discard overgrown plants.
Prone to attack by mealy bugs.

HYDRANGEA
MACROPHYLLA
(China and Japan)

Height 60cm (2ft)
Light Indirect
Temperature Cool: min 7°C
(45°F)
Humidity Dry

A well-known garden plant,
which looks equally effective
in the home. The large
rounded heads of white, pink
or blue flowers last up to six
weeks in early summer.

Care Water freely throughout
the summer. It is essential
to use softened water;
particularly for the blue
flowering varieties, because
their compost has been
specially 'blued' by the
chemical alum to increase
the acidity.

Grower's guide The plants
will not bloom inside for a
second season, but may be
placed outside. Cut flowering
shoots right back when
deadheading. Yellowing of
the veins is caused by
chlorosis.

HYPOCYRTA GLABRA
(South America)
Clog plant

Height 30cm (1ft)
Light Full, out of direct sun
Temperature Moderate: min 10°C (50°F)
Humidity High

A cheerful, spring- and summer-flowering plant, with shiny, dark green, succulent, oval-shaped foliage. Bright orange, slightly puffy-looking flowers grow along the entire length of the stems. Its slightly arching form makes it ideal for hanging baskets.

Care Water thoroughly during the growing season, but allow compost to dry out slightly before re-watering. Keep the compost on the dry side during winter. Feed monthly during the summer. Pot-on when necessary, in a peat-based compost.

Grower's guide Cut the stems back in autumn. Allow the plant to rest during the winter by placing it in a cool, but well-lit, position.

HYPOESTES SANGUINOLENTA
(Madagascar)
Polka dot plant

Height 46cm (1½ft)
Light Full light, out of direct sun
Temperature Moderate: min 13°C (55°F)
Humidity Moderate

Bright, low-growing plants, with small, olive green leaves, attractively smothered with pink spots.

Care Water thoroughly and evenly throughout the growing season, but avoid waterlogging and never let the plant sit in water. Give softened, tepid water.

Grower's guide Pinch out growing tips regularly to encourage bushy growth. The plants have a tendency to become straggly after one season and are better discarded.

IMPATIENS
(Africa)
Busy lizzie

Height 30-60cm (1-2ft)
Light Full light, out of direct sun
Temperature Moderate: min 13°C (55°F)
Humidity Low

These popular plants produce flowers throughout the summer, in shades ranging from red and salmon, to deep pink and white. The 'New Guinea' hybrids flower less profusely, but have attractive foliage.

Care Keep compost moist while the plant is flowering, but never waterlogged. Water sparingly during the dormant period, keeping compost just moist. Feed fortnightly during the summer. Plants flower most freely when pot-bound; pot-on when absolutely necessary, in a peat-based compost.

Grower's guide Pinch out growing tips frequently. Underwatering results in loss of leaves and wilting; stems collapse if overwatered. Spindly growth is usually due to hot, dull conditions. Flowers drop in low-lighting levels. Prone to attack by red spider mite.

JACARANDA MIMOSIFOLIA
(Australia)
Jacaranda

Height 1m (3ft)
Light Bright, with some sun
Temperature Moderate: min 13°C (55°F)
Humidity High

An elegant house plant, with fine, tree-like proportions. The lacy, fern-like, finely divided foliage makes it an excellent choice for a plant table or pedestal.

Care Keep the compost moist during the growing period, but allow it to dry out slightly between waterings. Water sparingly in winter. Always give tepid, softened water. Feed fortnightly during the summer. Pot-on when necessary in spring, using a peat-based compost.

Grower's guide The delicate leaflets will rapidly drop in dry atmospheres. Prone to attack by red spider mite.

JASMINUM POLYANTHUM
(China)
Jasmine

Height 3m (10ft)
Light Bright, with some sun
Temperature Moderate: min 7°C (45°F)
Humidity Low

A rampant climber, with fragrant, white, star-shaped flowers, which open from pink buds and appear through winter and spring. *J. primulinum* produces non-fragrant, semi-double, yellow flowers in the spring.

Care Water frequently during periods of rapid growth, but do not allow compost to become waterlogged. During the dormant period, water sparingly, but never allow compost to dry out. Use tepid water. Feed once a week throughout the growing season. Pot-on when necessary, in a loam-based compost (John Innes No 2).

Grower's guide Bring plant back into flower the following season by cutting back hard after flowering. Pinch out growing tips of plants grown for their foliage. Provide support for the stems. Buds and flowers will drop in dry atmospheres. Prone to attack by red spider mite.

KALANCHOË BLOSSFELDIANA 'Vulcan'
(Madagascar)

Height 15-25cm (6-10in)
Light Bright, with some sun
Temperature Moderate: min 7°C (45°F)
Humidity Dry

A flowering succulent, with fleshy, oval, bright green leaves, which have slightly-serrated edges. Long-lasting clusters of red, orange or yellow tubular flowers appear in late winter. Given sufficient light, the foliage will become slightly red.

Care Water thoroughly during the flowering period, but allow the compost to dry out slightly in between waterings. Cut back by one-third after flowering, and place the plant in a shady position. Keep the compost almost dry for four weeks, then return plant to a well-lit position and increase watering. Pot-on in a peat-based compost after this resting period.

Grower's guide Plants tend to become uncontrollably straggly after one year. Prone to attack by mealy bug.

LILIUM LONGIFLORUM
(Japan)
Easter lily

Height 1m (3ft)
Light Full light, out of direct sun
Temperature Cool: min 5°C (40°F)
Humidity Dry

Fragrant lilies, which flower in summer. The many large, trumpet-shaped blooms, with distinctive, golden anthers, are carried on a single, tall stem.

Care Keep compost moist at all times during the flowering period. Flowering time will be maximized by cool, night-time temperatures.

Grower's guide The bulb may be retained and re-started for the following year, but the growth will be less vigorous than on newly purchased bulbs.

MANETTIA INFLATA
(Subtropics)
Firecracker plant

Height 1.8m (6ft)
Light Bright, with some sun
Temperature Moderate: min 10°C (50°F)
Humidity Moderate

A colourful climbing plant, with thin, twining stems, which rapidly cover any available support. The tubular, waxy red flowers have yellow tips; they are borne in profusion throughout the summer.

Care Keep the compost evenly moist throughout the year. Reduce watering in winter. Feed fortnightly during the growing season and pot-on every year in spring. Use a peat-based compost.

Grower's guide Prune back lightly, after flowering. Encourage the growth of side shoots, by pinching out growing tips in early spring. Ensure minimum temperatures during the winter, to allow the plant an adequate rest. Train stems over wires or trelliswork, or allow them to trail.

MARANTA
(Brazil)
Prayer plant

Height 15-20cm (6-8in)
Light Indirect
Temperature Warm: min
13°C (55°F)
Humidity High

Spectacular foliage plants with attractively coloured veins and markings on their large, oval leaves. *M. leuconeura massangeana* has blackish-green leaves with silvery veins; *M. l. erythrophylla* has light green leaves with prominent red veins; and *M. l. kerchoveana*'s leaves have large brown blotches in between the veins.

Care During the growing period, water freely with tepid, softened water; water sparingly in winter. Give a fortnightly liquid feed during the summer. Pot-on annually, in a peat-based compost. Mature plants should be top-dressed.

Grower's guide The delicate foliage will burn in bright light. Dry conditions result in brown leaf tips and leaf fall. Water carefully and maintain even temperatures. Prone to attack by red spider mite.

MICROCOELUM
WEDDELIANUM syn. *Cocos weddeliana*
(Brazil)
Dwarf coconut palm

Height 30cm (1ft)
Light Indirect
Temperature Warm: min
16°C (60°F)
Humidity Very high

A delicate, compact palm, which demands constant heat and humidity. The slender fronds are dark green above and silvery on their undersides.

Care Water thoroughly during the summer, but allow the compost to dry out slightly before re-watering. Water cautiously in winter and avoid waterlogging at all times. Give a dilute liquid feed every two weeks from spring to autumn. Pot-on when the root ball is rising through the compost; use a peat-based mixture with some added sand.

Grower's guide A slow-growing palm, which takes twenty years to reach its maximum height of 1.8m (6ft).

MONSTERA DELICIOSA
(Mexico)
Swiss cheese plant

Height 2.4m (8ft) or more
Light Indirect
Temperature Warm: min
10°C (50°F)
Humidity Low

The bright, shiny, heart-shaped leaves develop holes and slashes as they enlarge and mature. The tall, lax stems should be supported by a permanently moistened, sphagnum moss-stick.

Care Water thoroughly during the growing season, but allow compost to slightly dry out in between waterings. Water sparingly during the winter. Feed fortnightly during the summer. Pot-on, when necessary, in a peat-based compost. Top-dress large plants annually.

Grower's guide Press the ends of the aerial roots into the moss-stick. The mature leaves will not develop their characteristic holes if conditions are too dry or too cold. Brown leaf tips and edges and yellowing patches are due to insufficient moisture, or low lighting. Stem rot during the winter is due to overwatering. Prone to attack by red spider mite in dry atmospheres.

MYRTUS COMMUNIS
(Mediterranean regions)
Myrtle

Height 60cm (2ft)
Light Bright, protect from strong sun
Temperature Cool: max
10°C (50°F)
Humidity Dry

An aromatic foliage plant, which may be grown as an untrimmed shrub, or clipped into shape. The small, glossy, oval-shaped leaves are an attractive mid-dark green. The fluffy, white flowers, with distinct yellow stamens, appear during the summer and are sometimes followed by purple-black fruits.

Care Water freely during the summer, but sparingly in winter, with softened, tepid water. Feed fortnightly during the growing season. Pot-on every other year in spring; use a peat-based compost.

Grower's guide Foliage may be trained at any time of year, making the plant ideal for indoor topiary. Grow in a well-ventilated spot and, if possible, place outside for a time during the summer.

NEOREGELIA CAROLINAE
'Tricolor'
(Brazil)

Height 23cm (9in)
Light Full light, out of
direct sun
Temperature Warm: min
16°C (60°F)
Humidity High

The spiny outer leaves of the
large rosette are a bright,
glossy-green, heavily striped
with rich yellow. When the
small, violet flower spike
starts to emerge from the
centre of the rosette in
summer, the leaves around
it turn a vivid red.

Care Keep the central vase
filled with water when the
plant is growing. Use
rainwater in hard water areas.
Empty and re-fill vase every
two to three months and keep
compost moist. During the
dormant period, vase and
compost should be just moist.
Empty vase if temperature
falls below winter minimum.
Feed monthly, either through
the vase or with a foliar spray.

Grower's guide Browning
leaf tips are normally due to
lack of humidity. The plant
will rot in wet conditions.
Prone to attack by scale
insects and mealy bug.

NEPHROLEPIS
EXALTATA
(Tropics)

Height 46-60cm (1½-2ft)
Light Indirect
Temperature Warm: min
10°C (50°F)
Humidity High

A group of fast-growing ferns
with large fronds. *N. exaltata*
has an upright habit, while
N. e. 'Bostoniensis' has
graceful, arching foliage
and is best displayed in a
hanging basket. Leaf edges
may be slightly twisted,
(*N. e.* 'Fluffy Ruffles') or
feathery (*N. e.* 'Whitmanii').
Runners, which will grow
young plantlets, rise from the
tops of the rhizome.

Care The compost must be
kept evenly moist, but never
waterlogged, throughout the
year. Water less during the
winter. Feed fortnightly
during the summer. Pot-on in
the spring, when the pot is
filled with roots, in equal
parts of John Innes No 2 and
peat.

Grower's guide Fronds will
yellow, and die back in hot,
dry conditions. Limp, wilting
fronds are caused by
overwatering. Cut out all
dead, and dying, fronds
entirely.

OXALIS CERNUA
(South Africa)
Bermuda buttercup

Height 23cm (9in)
Light Full, out of direct sun
Temperature Cool: min 5°C
(40°F)
Humidity Dry

This attractive garden
plant makes a wonderful
hanging display in a cool
conservatory. It has masses
of slightly succulent, bright
green, cloverlike foliage and
drooping umbels of simple-
petalled, yellow flowers,
which appear all summer
long.

Care During the summer,
allow the compost to dry out
slightly before re-watering.
Water cautiously in winter.
Feed monthly, while the
plant is in flower. Pot-on in
autumn, when the container
is full of the tiny bulbils.

Grower's guide Allow plenty
of ventilation during the
summer.

PACHYSTACHYS LUTEA
(Peru)
Lollipop plant

Height 30-46cm (1-1½ft)
Light Indirect
Temperature Moderate: min
13°C (55°F)
Humidity Low

Curious upright cones of
yellow flowering bracts, with
protruding white flowers,
grow above the dense dome
of foliage throughout the
summer. Large, oval, shiny,
green leaves, with prominent
veins, make *P. lutea* an
attractive foliage plant
during the winter months.

Care Keep the compost
permanently moist, but not
soggy, from spring to late
autumn. Water sparingly in
winter. Feed fortnightly
during the growing season.
Pot-on annually in the
spring. Use a peat-based
compost.

Grower's guide Cut back all
the stems by half at the start
of the growing season. Plants
tend to become straggly after
two to three years and are
better discarded. Leaf fall
normally indicates dry
compost. Prone to attack
by aphids.

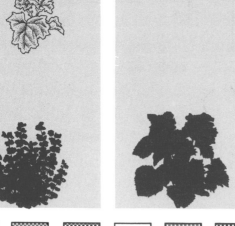

PELARGONIUM CRISPUM
(South Africa)
Scented leaved geranium

Height 60cm (2ft) or more
Light Bright, with some sun
Temperature Moderate: min 7°C (45°F)
Humidity Dry

This group of pelargoniums are grown for their distinctively-scented leaves. The leaves of *P. crispum* have a strong lemon fragrance. *P. graveolens* has rose-scented, grey-green leaves. *P. tormentosum* has the most beautiful pale green, velvety leaves; this peppermint-scented variety looks most effective when trained into a fan shape.

Care Water plants thoroughly, but allow compost to almost dry out in between waterings. Keep compost just moist during the winter. Feed fortnightly during the growing season. Pot-on when necessary in the spring (John Innes No 2). Remove dead flower heads immediately.

Grower's guide Place plants where foliage will be brushed against. Keep well-ventilated during the summer and away from cold windowsills during the winter.

PELARGONIUM DOMESTICUM
(South Africa)
Regal geranium

Height 37-60cm (15-24in)
Light Bright, with some sun
Temperature Moderate: min 10°C (50°F)
Humidity Dry

Showy pelargoniums with frilly, finely-serrated leaf edges and large heads of blooms, which appear during the spring. Colours tend to be subtle pinks and maroons, with deeper shades running along their veins.

Care Water plants thoroughly, when the compost has nearly dried out, during the growing season; and only sparingly in winter. Remove dead flower heads immediately, and never mist blooms. Pot-on, when the pot is filled with roots, in a loam-based compost (John Innes No 2).

Grower's guide Provide plenty of ventilation during the summer and avoid cold windowsills during the winter. *P. domesticum* is more susceptible to disease than *P. crispum* — particularly to blackleg disease, botrytis and oedema. Red leaves are due to low temperatures.

PELARGONIUM HORTORUM
(South Africa)
Geranium

Height 60-90cm (2-3ft)
Light Bright, with some sun
Temperature Moderate: min 7°C (45°F)
Humidity Dry

These popular 'zonal' varieties, have distinctive horseshoe marking on their leaves. They are tall-growing plants, with dense flower heads in shades of pink, red or white, which are held above the foliage on long stalks. Flowers may be double or single, and are borne in profusion throughout the summer.

Care Water thoroughly during the growing season, but allow compost to almost dry out before re-watering. Keep compost just moist in winter. Give a fortnightly liquid feed and pot-on only when absolutely necessary. Remove dead flower heads promptly to prevent plant setting seed. Never mist.

Grower's guide *P. hortorum* will react to unsuitable conditions in the same way as the other members of the group. In addition, it tends to shed its lower leaves; to prevent a leggy appearance, cut back hard in the spring.

PELARGONIUM PELTATUM
(South Africa)
Ivy-leafed geranium

Trailing 1m (3ft)
Light Bright, with some sun
Temperature Moderate: min 10°C (50°F)
Humidity Dry

A trailing variety that is ideal for hanging baskets; it has ivy-shaped leaves and large single or double blooms, which are freely borne from summer to autumn.

Care Water thoroughly, then allow compost to become moderately dry before re-watering. Water sparingly in winter; keeping the compost just moist. Give a fortnightly liquid feed during the growing season. Pot-on when absolutely necessary in spring, using John Innes No 2 potting compost.

Grower's guide Cut back in spring to force side shoots. Underwatering will result in the yellowing of firm leaves and in scorched edges. Avoid cold windowsills in cold weather; foliage will redden in cold conditions. Black leg disease, botrytis or oedema may occur.

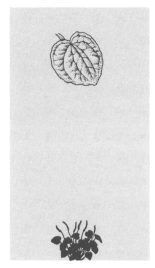

PELLAEA ROTUNDIFOLIA
(New Zealand)
Button fern

Height 46cm (1½ft)
Light Indirect
Temperature Moderate: min 10°C (50°F)
Humidity Moderate

This fern is ideal as ground cover. It has round, leathery leaflets on low-growing fronds and thrives in the humidity provided by other plants. However, it also looks very effective trailing down the sides of pots.

Care Keep compost moist throughout the year, but give less water during the dormant period. Feed fortnightly during the summer and pot-on in spring. Use a peat-based compost.

Grower's guide One of the most tolerant ferns for drier conditions, but mist around the plant in warm rooms to prevent fronds from browning.

PEPEROMIA CAPERATA
(South America)

Height 10-25cm (4-10in)
Light Full light, out of direct sun
Temperature Warm: min 10°C (50°F)
Humidity Very high

A low-growing, bushy plant with small, heart-shaped, purple-tinted, dark green leaves, which have very crinkled surfaces. *P. c.* 'Variegata' has distinct white margins. Creamy-white, red-stalked flower spikes grow high above the foliage during the summer.

Care Water cautiously with tepid water during the summer; allow the compost to dry out in between waterings. In winter, keep the compost almost dry. Water from beneath to avoid wetting the very delicate leaves. Feed monthly during the summer. These small-rooted plants will never exceed a 9cm (3½in) pot size.

Grower's guide Bottle gardens provide an ideal environment, i.e. constant temperature and high humidity. Allow maximum winter lighting levels.

PEPEROMIA MAGNOLIAEFOLIA
'Variegata'
(South America)
Desert privet

Height 20cm (8in)
Light Indirect
Temperature Warm: min 10°C (50°F)
Humidity Moderate

An upright, freely-branching plant with fleshy stems and succulent, oval leaves, coloured green and cream. Juvenile leaves are almost white.

Care Water sparingly during the growing season, allowing compost to almost dry out before re-watering. Keep the compost just moist during the winter. Always give soft, tepid water from below to avoid wetting the stems. Feed monthly during the summer. Re-pot when necessary in a peat-based compost.

Grower's guide Pinch out the growing tips regularly. Avoid draughts at all times and provide constant levels of heat and humidity. Brown leaf tips are the result of a sudden drop in temperature.

PEPEROMIA SCANDENS
'Variegata'
(South America and West Indies)
Trailing peperomia

Spread 3m (10ft)
Light Full light, out of direct sun
Temperature Warm: min 16°C (60°F)
Humidity Moderate

The fleshy, heart-shaped leaves are about 5cm (2in) in length; and have a pale cream colouring, which becomes light green with cream margins. This variety may be grown as a trailing plant, or trained upwards.

Care Water sparingly at all times. Allow the compost to almost dry out in between waterings, and keep almost dry in winter. Use tepid water during the winter and always avoid damp conditions. Feed monthly during the growing season. Pot-on annually, but top-dress after a 10cm (4in) pot size has been reached.

Grower's guide Never overwater, the plant is difficult to establish during the early stages, and will not tolerate excessive damp during cold periods; established plants are easier to maintain.

PHILODENDRON BIPINNATIFIDUM
(Brazil)
Tree philodendron

Height 1m (3ft)
Light Indirect
Temperature Warm: min 13°C (55°F)
Humidity Low

A handsome philodendron, which displays well in hanging baskets. Deeply-incised, mature leaves on long fleshy stalks rise from a central stem. The juvenile leaf form, which appears for two years, is heart-shaped.

Care Water thoroughly during the summer; allow the compost to dry out slightly before re-watering. During the winter, keep compost just moist. Feed monthly during the summer. Pot-on, when necessary, in a peat-based compost. Place crocks at the base of the pot. Top-dress mature plants annually. Sponge leaves regularly with tepid water.

Grower's guide Stems will rot if waterlogged. Stunted mature foliage is probably due to inadequate warmth and humidity. Wrap sphagnum moss around aerial roots in extreme conditions. Prone to attack by red spider mite.

PHILODENDRON ERUBESCENS 'Burgundy'
(Colombia)

Height 1.8m (6ft)
Light Full light, out of direct sun
Temperature Moderate: min 13°C (55°F)
Humidity Moderate

This slower-growing philodendron is outstanding for its copper-red juvenile leaves, which are carried on purple leafstalks. Their arrow-shaped form is retained in maturity.

Care Water thoroughly during the growing season, but allow the compost to dry out slightly in between waterings during the winter. Feed fortnightly from spring to late autumn. Pot-on every two years, in a peat-based compost, until a 25cm (10in) pot size is reached; thereafter top-dress annually. Allow maximum light during the winter to encourage leaf colouring.

Grower's guide Press the aerial roots into a permanently moistened sphagnum moss-stick, which will also provide the necessary support for the tall stems. Avoid draughts, fluctuating temperatures and overwatering in winter.

PHILODENDRON HASTATUM
(Brazil)
Elephant's ear philodendron

Height 1.5m (5ft)
Light Indirect
Temperature Moderate: min 13°C (55°F)
Humidity Moderate

A moderate climber, with shiny, mid-green, arrow-shaped leaves. *P. andreanum*, known in its juvenile form as *P. melanochryson*, has similarly shaped foliage, with a velvety, darker green finish. The leaves hang vertically from the stem. It is a more demanding plant, which requires a minimum temperature of 18°C (65°F).

Care Water thoroughly during the summer, but allow the compost to dry out slightly before re-watering. Feed fortnightly throughout the summer. Pot-on, when necessary, in a peat-based compost. Mature plants should be top-dressed.

Grower's guide Yellowing, dropping leaves and rotting stems are caused by overwatering. Grow plant up a permanently moist sphagnum moss-stick; this provides anchorage and moisture for the aerial roots.

PHILODENDRON PANDURAEFORME
(Brazil)
Fiddle leaf

Height 1.8m (6ft)
Light Indirect
Temperature Warm: min 13°C (55°F)
Humidity Moderate

A large-leafed climber, with bright, glossy green leaves, which are held out from the stem by long fleshy stalks. Mature leaves are narrow-waisted, but deeply lobed near their stalks; juvenile foliage tends to be more regular.

Care Water thoroughly and regularly from early spring to late autumn. Keep the compost just moist during the winter. Feed every two weeks during the growing season. Pot-on every two years in a peat-based compost. Mature plants should be top-dressed annually.

Grower's guide Train the stems up a permanently moistened sphagnum moss-stick, so that the aerial roots may be pressed into it. Peel off any faded leaves. Prone to attack by red spider mite.

PHILODENDRON SCANDENS
(Panama)
Sweetheart plant

Height 1.8m (6ft) or more
Light Indirect
Temperature Moderate:
10°C (50°F)
Humidity Low

A strong, evergreen climber, with mid-green, heart-shaped leaves and slender stems, which will climb or trail indefinitely unless pinched out.

Care Water compost evenly and well during the summer, but reduce watering during the dormant period. Feed fortnightly throughout the summer. Pot-on in a peat-based compost; normally every two years.

Grower's guide Weak, straggly growth is due to insufficient light. Regularly pinch out the growing tip to encourage the growth of side shoots. Support climbers with a moistened sphagnum moss-stick, which will provide moisture for the upper leaves.

PHOENIX CANARIENSIS
(Canary Islands)

Height 3m (10ft)
Light Indirect
Temperature Cool: min 7°C
(45°F)
Humidity Low

A dwarf member of the date palm, with many narrow, mid-green leaflets, which arch stiffly outwards. A robust, slow-growing plant, which retains its attractive appearance for many years.

Care Water frequently during the summer, but reduce watering in the dormant season; never allow the soil to remain saturated for long periods. Give fortnightly liquid feed throughout the summer. Pot-on in a loam-based compost (John Innes No 2), every second year. Line pot with broken crocks to ensure adequate drainage.

Grower's guide Provide an airy position during the summer, but avoid winter draughts. Clean the foliage by sponging with tepid water.

PILEA CADIEREI
(Vietnam)
Aluminium plant

Height 30cm (1ft)
Light Full light, out of direct sun
Temperature Warm: min
10°C (50°F)
Humidity Moderate

The plant forms a spreading mound of lightly corrugated, silver-splashed leaves. *P. c.* 'Nana' is a more compact form, which is better suited to warmer conditions.

Care Water thoroughly with tepid water, during periods of rapid growth, but avoid waterlogged conditions. Feed fortnightly during the summer and pot-on annually in a peat-based compost.

Grower's guide Cut back stems in spring and regularly pinch out the growing tips. Cold air and wet compost will cause serious leaf fall. Provide constant temperatures, avoid draughts and cold windowsills. The plant will become uncontrollably straggly after three to four years and should be discarded.

PILEA NUMMULARIFOLIA
(South America)
Creeping Charlie

Height Prostrate
Light Full light, out of direct sun
Temperature Warm: min
10°C (50°F)
Humidity Moderate

An attractive plant to grow in hanging baskets, or as ground cover in a light position. Tiny, yellowish-green, rounded leaves grow from the red, thread-like stems, which throw out roots as they grow.

Care Water well with tepid water during the growing season, but reduce watering in winter. Avoid waterlogging by allowing the compost to dry out slightly between waterings. Feed fortnightly during the summer. Pot-on annually in a peat-based compost.

Grower's guide Some leaves will be lost naturally during the winter, but heavy leaf fall is normally due to overwatering or to the use of cold water. Foliage will discolour in low lighting levels. Maintain constant levels of temperature.

PLATYCERIUM BIFURCATUM
(Australia)
Stag's horn fern

Height 45-75cm (1½-2½ft)
Light Full light, out of direct sun
Temperature Warm: min 10°C (50°F)
Humidity Moderate

An epiphytic fern, with two types of frond. The main fronds are ribbon-like for half their length, but then divide sharply to form antler-like shapes. They are a dark green, but their fine covering of silvery hairs gives them a grey-green appearance. The broad, fan-shaped fronds curl around the container and provide a natural anchor for the plant, while providing food for the main fronds.

Care Water and clean the plant by immersing it in a bucket of tepid water; weekly during the summer, fortnightly when the plant is dormant. Allow it to drain before re-hanging.

Grower's guide Avoid touching the leaf surfaces; the surface hairs will not re-grow. Never remove the decaying (infertile) lower fronds or the spores, which are borne on the underside of the main (fertile) fronds.

PLECTRANTHUS AUSTRALIS
(Australia)
Swedish ivy

Height 23cm (9in)
Light Full light, out of direct sun
Temperature Moderate: min 10°C (50°F)
Humidity Low

A small-leaved plant, which makes an attractive subject for a hanging basket.
P. australis has bright green, serrated, round leaves growing from long trailing stems; *P. coleoides* 'Marginatus' is less vigorous, with white margins around matt foliage. The cultivar 'Oertendahlii' has strongly defined, creamy-yellow veins on a bronze background.

Care During the growing season, water thoroughly whenever the compost begins to feel dry. Reduce watering in winter. Feed monthly during the summer and pot-on, in a peat-based compost, when roots are filling the pot.

Grower's guide Cut out straggly growths at any time and pinch out the growing tips in spring. Plants tend to become uncontrollably straggly, particularly if not given maximum light during the winter.

PLUMBAGO CAPENSIS
(South Africa)

Height 1-1.2m (3-4ft)
Light Full light, out of direct sun
Temperature Cool: min 7°C (45°F)
Humidity Low

Delightful, ice-blue clusters of simple-petalled flowers grow freely from the tips of the slender shoots throughout the summer.

Care Keep compost moist at all times, but water sparingly during the winter. Feed fortnightly during the summer. Grow in a well-ventilated spot; ensure good flowering by keeping plant cool throughout the winter and early spring. Pot-on annually in spring, using a loam-based compost (John Innes No 3).

Grower's guide Cut back in late winter, before the start of the growing season. If root knot eelworms attack, the growth rate will be considerably reduced. Provide some support for the tall stems.

PODOCARPUS MACROPHYLLUS
(Tropics and Subtropics)
Southern yew

Height 1.2m (4ft)
Light Bright, with some sun
Temperature Cool: min 5°C (40°F)
Humidity Dry

A compact bush that may be clipped to shape at any time. It has slender, leathery leaves, which are a yellowish-green on top and bluish-green underneath. A slow-growing, draught-tolerant plant, it makes an excellent choice for the cool conservatory, or hallway.

Care Keep the compost moist at all times, but never waterlogged; reduce watering during the winter. Feed monthly during the growing season. Pot-on, or top-dress, annually, in spring. Use a rich, loam-based mixture, with plenty of crocks in the base of the pot. Always keep the pot in proportion to the root ball; small plants in large pots will become easily waterlogged.

Grower's guide Avoid high temperatures and provide maximum ventilation during the summer.

POLYANTHUS
(British Isles)

Height 15-20cm (6-8in)
Light Full light, out of direct sun
Temperature Cool: max 16°C (60°F)
Humidity Dry

Taller-growing forms of *Primula vulgaris*, which provide welcome colour throughout winter and early spring. There are many hybrids — the Pacific strain makes particularly attractive plants, with large flowers in brilliant shades of blue, yellow, red, pink and white.

Care Keep the compost evenly moist during the flowering season; never feed the plant when it is in flower. Plant outside after flowering, where it will continue to flower and increase each year.

Grower's guide Never leave plants on cold windowsills; deadhead frequently to prevent plant setting seed.

PTERIS CRETICA
(South West Europe, India, Japan)
Ribbon fern

Height 30-46cm (1-1½ft)
Light Indirect
Temperature Warm: min 7°C (45°F)
Humidity High

Delicate ferns, with mid-green, ribbon-like, slightly serrated leaflets, which arch from upright, thread-like stems. *P. c.* 'Albolineata' has slightly wider fronds with very pale centres.

Care Keep compost evenly moist throughout the year; reduce the frequency of watering during the winter. Feed fortnightly during the summer. Pot-on in spring, when necessary. Use equal quantities of sand, peat-based compost and moss-peat.

Grower's guide Promptly remove dead, or damaged, fronds at their base. Avoid sources of direct heat, gas fumes and draughts. The constant conditions provided by a bottle garden are ideal.

RHAPIS EXCELSA
(Asia)
Lady palm

Height 1.5m (5ft)
Light Indirect
Temperature Moderate: min 10°C (50°F)
Humidity Moderate

Clusters of wide, fan-shaped, shiny leaves are held out on long stems, which branch off the main fibrous stem.

Care Keep the compost evenly moist during the growing season; reduce watering in winter. Feed fortnightly during the summer and pot-on overcrowded plants at the start of the growing season. Use a peat-based compost.

Grower's guide Sponge leaves regularly with soft, tepid water. In common with other palms, *R. excelsa* has a long root system and should be grown in tall flowerpots.

RHIPSALIDOPSIS GAERTNERI
(Brazil)
Easter cactus

Height 30-46cm (1-1½ft)
Light Full light, out of direct sun
Temperature Warm: min 13°C (55°F)
Humidity High

An epiphytic, forest cactus with flattened, succulent stems, which are divided into dull green, pad-like sections. Scarlet, trumpet-shaped flowers appear profusely in the spring.

Care Water liberally when flowering, but allow compost to dry out slightly before re-watering. After flowering, place outside in a shady area to develop new pads. In early autumn, bring plant inside to a cool position, watering only when absolutely necessary. Increase watering slightly in late winter and place plant in its flowering position. Increase watering as the buds begin to form. Always give softened water. Feed weekly as buds are forming. Re-pot annually after flowering, in equal parts of leaf mould and fine gravel.

Grower's guide Never move plant once flower buds have formed.

RHOEO DISCOLOR
(Central America)
Boat lily

Height 30cm (1ft)
Light Indirect
Temperature Moderate: min
7°C (45°F)
Humidity Moderate

Stiff, sword-shaped, fleshy
leaves grow from a short
stem; metallic, dark green
above and purple below. Tiny
white flowers lie cradled
within the leafy bracts. In
time, the lower leaves fall to
reveal a squat stem. If the
plant is being grown for
individual display, remove all
side shoots; but the rather
attractive arching forms
should be retained for
hanging baskets.

Care Keep compost moist at
all times; reduce frequency of
watering during the winter.
Give a fortnightly liquid feed
during the summer. Pot-on,
when necessary, in spring,
using a peat-based compost.

Grower's guide Remove dead
flowers and leaves promptly.
Allow maximum light during
the winter, but avoid
draughts.

RHOICISSUS
RHOMBOIDEA
(South Africa)
Grape ivy

Height 1.2-1.8m (4-6ft)
Light Indirect
Temperature Cool: min 7°C
(45°F)
Humidity Low

A vigorous climbing plant,
which is ideal for difficult,
shaded corners. Densely-
growing dark green, shiny
leaves are arranged in groups
of three.

Care Water freely in summer;
sparingly in winter. Avoid
waterlogging at all times.
Feed fortnightly during the
growing season. Mist leaves
occasionally in hot, dry
conditions. Pot-on annually
until a 23cm (9in) pot size
is reached. Top-dress
thereafter.

Grower's guide Give
support, if growing plant as
a climber. Pinch out leaves
to encourage bushy growth.
Brown patches on leaves
result from exposure to direct
sun. Shrivelled yellow or
falling leaves indicate
overwatering. Brown leaves
are due to lack of water.

RUELLIA MACRANTHA
(Brazil)
Christmas pride

Height 1m (3ft)
Light Full light, out of
direct sun
Temperature Warm: min
13°C (55°F)
Humidity Moderate

Tall, shrubby plants that
make splendid winter-
flowering specimens. The
handsome, dark green leaves
are long and pointed. Large
clusters of trumpet-shaped,
rose-purple blooms appear at
the tips of the shoots.

Care Water thoroughly,
throughout the year; decrease
the amount only slightly
during the winter. Feed
fortnightly while the buds are
forming. Prune to within 8cm
(3in) of the base when
flowering is over and re-pot
in a peat-based compost.

Grower's guide Pinch out
the growing tips of young
plants to maintain a bushy
habit. Yellowing and falling
leaves are usually the result
of insufficient moisture or
humidity.

SAINTPAULIA
IONANTHA
(South Africa)
African violet

Height 8-10cm (3-4in)
Light Full light, out of
direct sun
Temperature Warm: min
16°C (60°F)
Humidity Moderate

Delicate purple-blue flowers,
with yellow eyes, rest on a
rosette of soft, mid-green
foliage. There are many
named cultivars, which
bloom in a wide variety
of colours.

Care Keep the compost
permanently moist, but never
soggy. Give tepid water and
feed mature plants fortnightly
during the growing season.

Grower's guide Always water
from below to avoid wetting
the fragile, easily-marked
foliage and flowers. Remove
dead flowers with their stalks,
and the suckers that form
around the base of plants.

SANSEVIERIA TRIFASCIATA 'Laurentii'
(West Africa)
Mother-in-law's tongue

Height 46cm (1½ft)
Light Full light, out of direct sun
Temperature Moderate: min 10°C (50°F)
Humidity Dry

These plants are tough succulents that will survive almost any conditions. They are rather slow-growing. The sword-like stems are a mottled, dark green with creamy yellow edges.

Care Water moderately during the growing season, allowing the compost to dry out in between waterings. During the winter, water only once every two months. Avoid wetting the centre of the plant. Feed fortnightly during the growing season and pot-on when necessary. Use a peat-based compost.

Grower's guide Rotting at the base, yellowing leaves and dying back are normally due to overwatering in winter. If the leaves curl, increase watering.

SAXIFRAGA SARMENTOSA 'Tricolor'
(China)
Mother of thousands

Height 30cm (1ft)
Light Full light, out of direct sun
Temperature Moderate: min 7°C (45°F)
Humidity Low

Thread-like runners, bearing tiny plantlets, cascade from the parent plant. The long stemmed, furry leaves are veined silvery-grey, with pink undersides and edges. Small white, starry flowers appear in summer.

Care Water the plants freely during the growing season, but sparingly in winter. Feed fortnightly during the growing season. Pot-on every other year in spring, using a loam-based mixture.

Grower's guide Young plantlets may be detached and potted-up separately at re-potting time. If the leaves begin to yellow, reduce watering and check the drainage. Increase watering and/or humidity, if the runners turn brown.

SCHEFFLERA ACTINOPHYLLA
(Australasia)
Umbrella tree

Height 2m (6½ft)
Light Full light, out of direct sun
Temperature Moderate: min 13°C (55°F)
Humidity Moderate

Handsome feature plant with dark, glossy-green foliage. Long leaflets grow in radiating groups on long leaf-stalks, and increase in number as the plant matures.

Care Provide maximum light during the winter. Keep compost evenly moist throughout the growing season, but reduce watering during the winter. Feed from late spring to the end of summer. Encourage growth by re-potting annually until it is in a 20cm (8in) pot; thereafter top-dress every alternate year. Use a peat-based compost.

Grower's guide The loss of the lower leaves is normal on mature plants. Prone to attack by scale insects.

SCHLUMBERGERA × BUCKLEYII
(Brazil)
Christmas cactus

Height 15-23cm (6-9in)
Light Full light, out of direct sun
Temperature Warm: min 13°C (55°F)
Humidity Low

This popular forest cactus has cerise, trumpet-shaped flowers, which may appear at any time during the winter. The freely-branching, succulent stems are jointed into pads with distinct tooth edges. Other hybrids flower in shades of mauve, red, pink and white.

Care Water freely when the plant is in bud or flower; reduce watering in spring. Allow compost to almost dry out in between waterings. Harden plant off during the summer by placing it outside in a cool, shady spot. In autumn, bring it inside again, watering cautiously until the buds appear. Feed weekly from bud formation until flowering begins. Re-pot after flowering, in equal parts of loam, peat and leaf-mould.

Grower's guide Never move plant once buds have formed.

SCINDAPSUS AUREUS
(Solomon Islands)
Devil's ivy

Height 2m (6½ft)
Light Full, out of direct sun
Temperature Warm: min
13°C (55°F)
Humidity Moderate

These variegated climbers
have two distinct leaf forms.
The mature leaves are long
and heart-shaped, coloured
bright green with strong
yellow markings. The young
leaves are small, broad and
spear-shaped.

Care Keep the compost
evenly moist throughout the
growing season, but slightly
drier during the winter. Feed
monthly during the summer.
Pot-on young plants when
necessary; normally every two
to three years. Top-dress
plants over 1.2m (4ft), every
two years.

Grower's guide Limp,
curled leaves indicate low
temperatures. Increase
watering if leaves develop
spots and brown edges. Leaf
tips will shrivel in high
humidity. Yellowing, falling
leaves and rotting stems are
due to overwatering.

SEDUM MORGANIANUM
(Mexico)
Burro's tail

Trailing 30-60cm (1-2ft)
Light Bright
Temperature Moderate:
13°C (55°F)
Humidity Dry

A curiously attractive,
trailing epiphyte. The
stems are composed of tiny,
densely-packed, grey-green,
succulent leaves and look
very much like thick ropes.
A few small clusters of red
flowers may hang from their
tips in spring.

Care Water freely in summer,
but keep compost almost dry
during the winter. Feed
monthly and pot-on, when
necessary, in the spring.
Use equal quantities of
loam-based compost and
sand; cover the surface
with fine gravel.

Grower's guide
S. morganianum may also be
grown on a piece of cork
bark. Carefully wrap
sphagnum moss around the
roots before attaching the
plant. Completely immerse
pot in water whenever the
moss is dry.

SELAGINELLA APUS
(South America)
Creeping moss

Height Prostrate
Light Indirect
Temperature Warm: min
13°C (55°F)
Humidity Very high

These delicate mound-
forming plants, with their
tiny fronds, require stable,
very humid conditions.
S. apus grows particularly well
in the closed conditions of a
bottle garden.

Care Keep the compost
constantly moist and stand
the pots in containers of
moist peat or sphagnum moss;
or, grow the plants in bottle
gardens. Wide flat containers
will provide a suitable area
for the plant to spread over.
Pot-on in the spring, when a
larger surface is needed. Use
a peat-based compost. Give
the occasional weak feed.

Grower's guide Ensure lime-
free conditions and never
mist the plant — the foliage
is easily marked. Shrivelled,
browning leaves are
invariably caused by hot, dry
temperatures. Move plants to
a shadier position if pale
yellow leaves develop.

SENECIO CRUENTUS
(Canary Islands)
Cineraria

Height 45cm (1½ft)
Light Full light, out of
direct sun
Temperature Cool: min 7°C
(45°F)
Humidity Moderate

Winter- and spring-flowering
house plants, with masses of
daisy-like flowers almost
covering the soft, heart-
shaped foliage. There are
many varieties and hybrids,
with single, semi-double
or double blooms in blue,
purple, red, pink, white and
bicolours. Plants are grown in
succession to flower through
winter to mid-summer.

Care Water frequently,
allowing compost to dry out
slightly before re-watering.
Feed fortnightly from bud
formation to flowering.
Discard plant after flowering.

Grower's guide Plants
normally collapse as a result
of overwatering. Never allow
the compost to become
waterlogged. Remove dead
flowers immediately. In hot
conditions the leaves will
yellow and the flowering
period will be reduced.
Remove dead leaves
promptly, as cinerarias are
very susceptible to botrytis.

SENECIO MACROGLOSSUS
'Variegatus'
(South Africa)
Cape ivy

Height 1m (3ft) or more
Light Full light, out of direct sun
Temperature Moderate: min 10°C (50°F)
Humidity Low

A vigorous, variegated climber or trailing plant, with ivy-shaped, fleshy foliage and small, white, daisy-like flowers. The similar form of *S. mikanoides* (the German ivy) has plain green leaves, which provide an excellent contrast if the two varieties are grown in association.

Care Keep compost moist, but never waterlogged throughout the summer; water sparingly in winter. Always use softened water. Feed fortnightly from late spring to the end of summer. Pot-on every two years in a loam-based compost (John Innes No 2), until a 25cm (10in) pot size is reached; top-dress thereafter.

Grower's guide Pinch out growing tips regularly to deter its straggly habit and encourage side shoots. Provide support if grown as a climber.

SENECIO ROWLEYANUS
(South Africa)
String-of-beads

Height Trailing to 60cm (2ft)
Light Bright, with full sun
Temperature Warm: min 16°C (60°F)
Humidity Dry

An unusual succulent, with small round leaves threaded like beads on the trailing stems. Clusters of small white flowers appear on short stalks in early winter.

Care Water well in spring and summer. Decrease after flowering, during the dormant period. Give monthly feeds during the growing season. Pot-on, when necessary, in a loam-based compost (John Innes No 2), with added sharp sand for drainage.

Grower's guide Generally trouble-free.

SETCREASEA PURPUREA
(Mexico)
Purple heart

Height 37cm (15in)
Light Bright, with some sun
Temperature Moderate: 10°C (50°F)
Humidity Low

A vibrantly-coloured, trailing plant, closely related to the tradescantias. The downy, narrow, purple leaves grow up to 15cm (6in) long. Clusters of three-petalled, pink blooms appear at the end of the branched stems during the summer.

Care Water freely when the compost feels dry during the summer, but keep it just moist in the winter. Feed monthly during the growing season. Re-pot annually in spring, using a peat-based compost.

Grower's guide Pinch out growing tips regularly in early spring to encourage bushy growth.

SINNINGIA SPECIOSA
'Fyfiana'
(Brazil)
Gloxinia

Height 30cm (1ft)
Light Full light, out of direct sun
Temperature Warm: min 16°C (60°F)
Humidity Moderate

Large, velvety, dark green leaves and huge trumpet-shaped blooms make a dazzling display during the summer. The frilly-edged flowers, in shades of red, purple, pink and white, last for two months or more.

Care Water thoroughly with tepid water, but always allow the compost to dry out before re-soaking. Water from beneath to avoid damaging the fragile flowers and foliage. Feed fortnightly from bud formation to the end of the flowering period. The foliage dies back in autumn.

Grower's guide Remove dead flowers immediately to prevent rotting of delicate foliage. Increase humidity if buds fail to open. Tuber will rot if compost is waterlogged. Lack of light or use of cold water results in pale, elongated leaves. Avoid draughts. Store tubers and re-start in spring.

SOLANUM CAPSICASTRUM
(Brazil)
Winter cherry

Height 30-46cm (1-1½ft)
Light Bright, with some sun
Temperature Cool: min 7°C (45°F)
Humidity Low

A bushy plant, which bears large, cherry-like berries in the winter. The fruits ripen from dark green, through yellow to red, and last until early spring. Tiny white flowers appear in mid-summer. Although the plant is normally bought as an annual, it may be grown for a number of years.

Care Keep compost moist at all times. Place the plant outside during the summer to encourage flowering. Alternatively, regularly mist the flowerbuds. Feed fortnightly during the summer. Pot-on annually in spring, using a peat-based compost.

Grower's guide The berries are poisonous. Overwatering will result in leaf drop. In poor light or dry atmospheres the berries will fall.

SPARMANNIA AFRICANA
(South Africa)
House lime

Height 1m (3ft)
Light Full light, out of direct sun
Temperature Cool: min 7°C (45°F)
Humidity Low

Beautiful, soft, pale green foliage makes *S. africana* a perfect foil for group planting. The leaves are roughly heart-shaped and may grow up to 15cm (6in) across. Large, white-petalled flowers, with long golden stamens, normally appear on two-year-old plants. There are two flowering periods — early spring and early autumn.

Care Keep compost moist at all times. Daily watering may be necessary on hot summer days, but avoid overwatering in winter. Feed weekly from spring to early autumn. Young plants may need potting-on twice yearly. Use a loam-based compost (John Innes No 3).

Grower's guide Regularly check moisture content of compost. Stand plants outside in warm rain to clean the foliage.

SPATHIPHYLLUM WALLISII
(Colombia)
Peace lily

Height 23-30cm (9-12in)
Light Indirect
Temperature Cool: min 10°C (50°F)
Humidity Moderate

Glossy, dark green, lanceolate leaves grow on long, slender stems directly from the compost. Creamy-white flower heads, surrounded by white spathes, are held high above the foliage on delicate stems throughout the summer. 'Mauna Loa' is a taller, more majestic hybrid, but it requires more care.

Care Keep the compost moist at all times. Water freely and frequently during the summer, but reduce watering in winter. Feed every ten days through summer and early autumn. Clean foliage regularly with moistened cotton wool. Pot-on annually in a peat-based compost, until a 13cm (5in) pot size has been reached; top-dress thereafter.

Grower's guide Strong summer sun, draughts and winter cold will damage the plant. Prone to attack by red spider mite.

STEPHANOTIS FLORIBUNDA
(Madagascar)
Madagascar jasmine

Height 3m (10ft)
Light Full light, with shading from bright sun
Temperature Moderate: 13°C (55°F)
Humidity Low

A vigorous climbing plant, with dark green, glossy leaves and clusters of very fragrant, waxy, white flowers, which may appear at any time from late spring to early autumn.

Care Water thoroughly during the growing season, as soon as the compost feels dry and spray with tepid water every few days. Water sparingly in winter. Feed fortnightly from spring to early autumn and pot-on every year in a peat-based compost.

Grower's guide Train the stems up wires or around a hoop. Avoid cold draughts and sudden changes in conditions. During the winter, provide cool temperatures and bright light. Never move or turn plant when in flower. Cut out older stems after flowering. Prone to attack by mealy bugs and scale insects.

STRELITZIA REGINAE
(South Africa)
Bird of paradise

Height 90cm (3ft)
Light Bright, with some sun
Temperature Moderate: min 10°C (50°F)
Humidity Low

An exotic house plant, with brilliant orange and blue flower heads, which emerge from the tops of tall sturdy stems in spring, and last for several weeks. Large, leathery, paddle-shaped leaves form a large fan which surrounds the flower heads.

Care During the summer, water thoroughly whenever the compost begins to dry out. Reduce watering during the winter. Feed monthly in the growing season. Re-pot only when absolutely necessary, until a 20cm (8in) pot size has been reached; top-dress thereafter.

Grower's guide S. reginae flowers more freely when pot-bound. Give cool, bright winter conditions and some protection from burning summer sun.

STREPTOCARPUS ×
HYBRIDUS
(South Africa)
Cape primrose

Height 23-30cm (9-12in)
Light Full light, out of direct sun
Temperature Moderate: min 10°C (50°F)
Humidity Moderate

Delicate, trumpet-shaped flowers are borne on slender stems above the rosette of large, wrinkled, oval leaves. There are many hybrids, which bloom in shades of pink, blue, purple, red or white, from early summer to autumn.

Care Water freely during spring and summer, whenever the compost begins to dry out. Water from below to avoid wetting the easily-damaged foliage and flowers. Keep compost just moist during the winter. Feed every ten days from early summer to end of flowering. Pot-on annually in spring, using a peat-based compost.

Grower's guide Yellowing, rotting leaves are caused by direct watering. Always mist around the plant when improving humidity. Poor flowering is due to insufficient light.

STROMANTHE AMABILIS
(Tropical America)

Height 30cm (1ft)
Light Indirect
Temperature Warm: min 13°C (55°F)
Humidity High

The vividly patterned, rounded leaves are marked with a darker tone of green in a clear herringbone pattern. The undersides are greyish-green. S. sanguinea has large leaves; dark green and white above, maroon below.

Care During the growing period, water freely with tepid, softened water; keep the compost almost dry in winter. Give a fortnightly liquid feed during the summer. Pot-on annually, in a peat-based compost; top-dress mature plants.

Grower's guide Bright light will burn the foliage. Leaf tips will brown in dry conditions. Watering must be carefully monitored and even temperatures maintained. Bottle gardens provide an ideal environment.

SYNGONIUM
PODOPHYLLUM
(Mexico and Panama)
Goose foot plant

Height 1.2m (4ft) or more
Light Full light, out of direct sun
Temperature Moderate: min 16°C (60°F)
Humidity Moderate

The leaf shape and form of this attractive plant change dramatically in maturity. Juvenile plants have mottled, green and silvery-white, arrow-shaped leaves, which grow on sturdy stems directly from the compost. With age, the plant develops stems with aerial roots. The leaves lose their variegation and become lobed, before dividing into leaflets, with an overall length of up to 30cm (1ft).

Care Keep soil moist, but not waterlogged, throughout the summer. Water sparingly in winter. Feed fortnightly in late spring and summer. Pot-on every two years in a peat-based compost.

Grower's guide To retain juvenile foliage remove climbing stems as they appear. Provide support for climbers. Cool, dry atmospheres result in sudden wilting and shrivelling. Very prone to attack from aphids.

TETRASTIGMA VOINIERIANUM
(China)
Chestnut vine

Height 2.4m (8ft) or more
Light Full light, out of direct sun
Temperature Moderate: min 10°C (50°F)
Humidity Low

A rampant climber, with chestnut-like leaves and strong tendrils, which can grow 1m (3ft) or more each year. Greenish-yellow flowers appear on mature plants.

Care Keep compost moist throughout the year, but reduce frequency of watering during the winter. Feed fortnightly throughout the growing period. Pot-on annually in spring, until a 30cm (1ft) pot size is reached; thereafter top-dress. Use a loam-based compost (John Innes No 3), placing crocks in base of pot.

Grower's guide Regularly pinch out growing tips to encourage side shoots. Provide strong support. Brown patches on leaves are due to direct exposure to sunlight. Reduce watering if leaves shrivel, yellow or fall. Mildew is due to waterlogged conditions. Dry, brown leaves are caused by dry air.

TILLANDSIA CAPUT-MEDUSAE
(North and South America)
Medusa's head air plant

Height 15cm (6in)
Light Full light, out of direct sun
Temperature Warm: min 16°C (60°F)
Humidity Moderate

One of a large and varied genus of dry-growing bromeliads, *T. caput-medusae* has upright-growing, twisted and tangled leaves. Their grey-green colouring comes from a layer of tiny, woolly scales, or trichomes. Flowers are blue, with red bracts.

Care Mount on coral, bark or wood, using a special fixative, or attach to a bromeliad tree. Spray regularly (at least once a day in high temperatures), with rainwater or soft water. Add a little vinegar to water in hard water areas. During spring and summer, give a very dilute monthly feed, in the form of a foliar spray.

Grower's guide Aim to balance humidity with good ventilation; damp, airless conditions can cause rotting. Avoid direct sunlight. Spray during the day so that the plant can dry before the temperature falls at night.

TOLMEIA MENZIESII
(Western United States)
Piggy-back plant

Height 15cm (6in)
Light Full light, out of direct sun
Temperature Moderate: min 5°C (40°F)
Humidity Low

A compact plant with downy, maple-like foliage, which forms an attractive mound. Small plantlets grow from the base of the leaves and appear to sit on their surfaces. Pink-flushed, white flower spikes grow above the foliage in mid-summer.

Care Water thoroughly during the summer, but sparingly during the dormant period. Feed once a week in late spring and summer. Pot-on annually in spring, using a peat-based compost.

Grower's guide Ventilate the room well during the summer. Tolmeias prefer a well-lit situation, but will tolerate shade. Prone to attack by red spider mite.

TRADESCANTIA BLOSSFELDIANA
'Variegata'
(Argentina)
Tradescantia

Height 30cm (1ft) or more
Light Full light, out of direct sun
Temperature Moderate: min 7°C (45°F)
Humidity Low

Tradescantia are popular trailing plants, which will survive in most conditions, but only look their best when grown in a strong light. *T. b.* 'Variegata' is a particularly good cultivar. It has a rather upright habit and attractive leaves, striped in green and cream, with purple undersides.

Care Water freely during the summer, but allow compost to dry out slightly in between waterings. Water sparingly when dormant. Feed fortnightly during spring and summer. Pot-on annually in a peat-based compost.

Grower's guide Pinch out growing tips frequently and any plain green leaves, which may appear. Leaves will tend to lose their fine variegation in poor lighting levels. Discard uncontrollably straggly plants.

 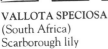

VALLOTA SPECIOSA
(South Africa)
Scarborough lily

Height 46cm (1½ft)
Light Bright, with some sun
Temperature Moderate: min 7°C (45°F)
Humidity Low

An autumn-flowering member of the Amaryllis family, each tall, fleshy stem carries umbels of four to ten vivid scarlet, trumpet-shaped blooms, with golden anthers. The long, narrow leaves are evergreen and provide continuing interest after the flowers have died.

Care During the summer and while the plant is flowering, water thoroughly, but allow compost to almost dry out before re-watering. Water cautiously through winter and spring. Feed monthly during the summer until the flowers have faded. Top-dress every year, but pot-on only when the bulbs are breaking out of the pot. Use a mixture of loam, sand and leaf-mould.

Grower's guide Allow the plant to rest over winter in cool temperatures. Remove dead flower heads and yellowing leaves promptly.

VRIESIA SPLENDENS
(South America)
Flaming sword

Height 46cm (1½ft)
Light Indirect
Temperature Warm: min 18°C (65°F)
Humidity Moderate

A terrestrial and epiphytic bromeliad, with typical rosette form and water vase. The thick, strap-like, glossy leaves are green, cross-banded with purple. A sword-shaped stem rises from the centre to a height of about 60cm (2ft), carrying a sheath of overlapping red bracts and yellow flowers.

Care During the growing season, use tepid, softened water to maintain an evenly moist compost and a full central vase. Water the compost sparingly during the winter. Add a diluted liquid feed to the vase once a month, during spring and summer, but not when the plant is flowering. Pot-on only when the roots are completely filling the pot, in equal parts of peat, sphagnum moss and sand.

Grower's guide Leaf tips will brown in dry atmospheres. Direct exposure to sun will result in brown patches on the foliage.

YUCCA ALOIFOLIA
(United States)
Spanish bayonet

Height 1.2-1.8m (4-6ft)
Light Bright, with some sun
Temperature Cool: min 7°C (45°F)
Humidity Dry

This house plant may be found in two forms: Y. elephantipes is the young form, with sword-shaped, spiky leaves growing from a central stem; the more familiar Y. aloifolia has young plants sprouting from sawn up sections of the mature stem.

Care Water thoroughly during the summer, but allow compost to dry out slightly before re-watering. Reduce watering in winter, keeping the compost just moist. Feed every fortnight during the spring and summer. Pot-on every year in spring, using a clay pot and a loam-based compost; the weight will provide a stable base for this rather top-heavy plant.

Grower's guide Brown tips on leaves indicate lack of water. Prone to attack by mealy bug and scale insects.

ZEBRINA PENDULA
(Mexico)
Wandering sailor

Trailing 46cm (1½ft)
Light Full light, out of direct sun
Temperature Moderate: 10°C (50°F)
Humidity Low

A more shade-tolerant relative of the tradescantia, its stems have the attractive habit of trailing downwards to cover the pot and then flicking upwards again. The wide leaves are richly striped with green, silver and purple above and are bright purple below.

Care Water freely during the growing period, but allow the compost to dry out slightly before re-watering. Water sparingly in winter. Give fortnightly liquid feed during the summer and pot-on annually in a peat-based compost.

Grower's guide Pinch out growing tips regularly to encourage bushy growth. Remove any plain green leaves and move plant to a brighter area.

►PLANT CARE◄

Take the time to care for your plants, and they will reward you by providing a continued source of pleasure. There is nothing more enjoyable than helping a plant to flourish and then watching the exciting growth of new foliage and flowers. The more you study plants, the easier it will be to identify their needs. Beginners are often slightly unnerved by the lack of many obvious rules for house plant care, but, if these did exist, then the breathtaking range of varieties you can grow would not. All plants need light, water, air and warmth to manufacture the food which they need for growth, but the exact amount varies and should always be a careful balance between the conditions in a plant's natural habitat and its present indoor environment.

LIGHTING LEVELS

Although all house plants need light, some are more tolerant of shady positions than others. It is not surprising, therefore, that many of the most successful house plants originate from sub-tropical and tropical areas, where they live in the filtered light conditions of the forest; for it is these regions that most closely reflect the lighting levels of the average interior. However, the range of house plants is not limited to these semi-shade lovers, and, in sharp contrast, there are the succulents from hot desert regions which thrive in bright conditions, while the more moderate flowering and bulbous plants from the temperate regions need sunshine in order to flower, but tolerate shadier locations at other times.

The importance of considering the requirements of each individual plant should never be underestimated; for unless its cultural demands are met and it is positioned where it will receive adequate lighting, it will fail to fulfil expectations. Deprive either variegated foliage, or flowering, plants of good, bright light and there will appear little reason to include them in a collection. The variegated leaves, with their limited supplies of essential chlorophyll, will either react

by reverting to plain green or, worse still, be entirely dropped by the plant. Fortunately the fine colouring may be regained when a brighter light is re-introduced; but the flower drop caused by moving a flowering plant to a duller position is irretrievable. A good light for these plants is obviously essential, but never confuse this with strong, direct sunlight. Although bright windowsills are ideal for some succulents and pelargoniums, most plants will not tolerate the heating levels generated by the focusing of the sun's rays through glass.

The amount of light which a plant receives is sometimes just as important as the quality. Some flowering plants are strongly influenced by their exposure to daylight hours and growers use this to bring them into flower throughout the year. Kalanchoës, poinsettias, chrysanthemums, and the ubiquitous Christmas cacti are all winter-flowering plants which naturally produce their flowers during the shortest days, but they are often induced to flower earlier by artificially reducing their hours of light during other times of the year. Conversely, saintpaulias

flower earlier when exposed to long hours of light and will bloom most freely when given 14 hours in every 24.

Positioning guide

- Check in the plant directory for a particular plant's optimum position.
- Never move a plant when in bud or flower.
- Turn plants slightly at regular intervals to prevent uneven, lopsided growth.
- Check variegated plants regularly for good colouring.
- Move a plant to a brighter position if it develops long, weak stems and pale leaves.
- Always avoid the midday sun on clear summer days.

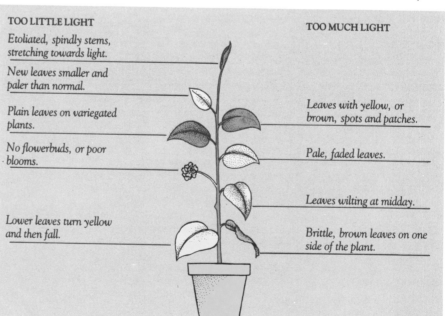

TOO LITTLE LIGHT

Etoliated, spindly stems, stretching towards light.

New leaves smaller and paler than normal.

Plain leaves on variegated plants.

No flowerbuds, or poor blooms.

Lower leaves turn yellow and then fall.

TOO MUCH LIGHT

Leaves with yellow, or brown, spots and patches.

Pale, faded leaves.

Leaves wilting at midday.

Brittle, brown leaves on one side of the plant.

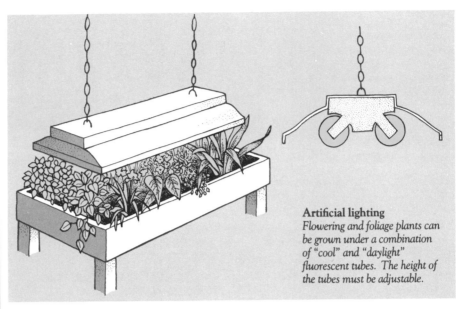

Artificial lighting
Flowering and foliage plants can be grown under a combination of "cool" and "daylight" fluorescent tubes. The height of the tubes must be adjustable.

ARTIFICIAL LIGHT

Artificial light may be used either to give a boost to light levels in poorly-lit areas, or as the only source of light, but for it to be effective it must be sufficiently intense without generating too much heat. Normal light bulbs would inevitably scorch the foliage, and although they are wonderful for highlighting displays, they should never be used as daylight substitutes. The most suitable lamps are either a combination of "cool" and "warm" fluorescent tubes, or high-pressure mercury arc lamps. The choice is largely a matter of taste and expense. Fluorescent tubes are longer and need a reflector to ensure that all the light is directed over the plants. Ideally they should also be adjustable in height to allow for plant growth; a factor which is unimportant when using arc lamps because they are sufficiently powerful to be ceiling-fixed. Arc lamps are cheaper to run, but much more expensive to buy. Whatever your choice it is always a good idea to control the light supply with a time switch – plants not only need their normal daylight hours, but also their nights.

TEMPERATURE

Each plant needs a minimum level of warmth to support its individual growth pattern, but it is much more important to balance temperature with the supply of light, water and humidity, for they are all interlinked. A plant grown in higher temperatures will use more water and demand higher levels of lighting than a plant grown in a cooler place, where growth will be less rapid.

The minimum temperature which a plant will tolerate varies. Many need cooler winter temperatures because low light conditions mean that they simply cannot manufacture enough food to support vigorous growth. Others need a cool winter rest period to ensure strong growth during the summer (such plants should always be placed in a cool, but frost-free area). Some plants, however, demand warmer conditions and although these must always be met, you must also ensure that the level of light is adequate.

Constant growing conditions are equally vital; for plants which are constantly re-adjusting to different temperatures, will never have sufficient reserves to develop strongly. A drop in night-time temperatures is quite natural for plants, but wildly fluctuating temperatures should always be avoided. Draughty positions are dangerous, because they create "stop-go" growing conditions, and the introduction of turbulent air increases the rate of water loss from the leaf surfaces, making watering very difficult to control. Close proximity of direct sources of heat will provide similarly uneven conditions.

Summer conditions should also be considered, for, while maintaining sufficiently high, even temperatures might be a problem during the winter, it is sometimes forgotten that many plants which originate from the temperate zones, such as the ivies and × *Fatshedera lizei*, need cool summers. Always ensure that these plants, as well as the many flowering varieties, have adequate supplies of fresh, cooling air.

Dos and don'ts
■ Never leave plants between curtains and windows on cold nights.
■ Avoid direct sources of heat and extreme fluctuations in temperature.
■ Minimize heat loss through large windows.
■ Never underestimate the intensity of heat generated through glass.
■ Water more frequently in higher temperatures and brighter light.

Temperature guide ▷
The minimum temperature which an indoor plant will tolerate varies. Most require a fairly constant temperature during the growing season, followed by a cooler rest period.

85°F (29°C) is the maximum temperature for most house plants, as long as extra humidity is provided.

75°F (24°C) is the maximum temperature if no extra humidity is provided.

60°F (16°C) is the minimum temperature for tender plants.

50-55°F (10-13°C) is the minimum for non-hardy plants.

40-45°F (5-7°C) is the minimum temperature for hardy plants.

HUMIDITY

Many care problems are the result of dry air, for this creates the ideal conditions for pests and diseases and so is most unsuitable for many plants. Plants are constantly losing water vapour through their leaves, in fact they rely on this transpiration to distribute their food supplies and to keep their stems rigid. This water loss is best utilized in growing plants together, as few plants are "built" to tolerate the heavy water losses caused by dry atmospheres. Humidity levels will be generally improved by installing electric humidifiers, or the units which are placed over radiators. The most simple solution.is to place small bowls of water around the room. Any of these measures will improve conditions for people and furniture as well as for the plants.

However, on a lesser scale, it is possible to concentrate solely on the areas immediately surrounding the plants. A group of plants can all be placed in one large container filled with constantly-moistened peat, or else rested on damp pebbles. Individual plants will need separate containers, but should be treated in the same way as the group. Climbers will always benefit from the extra humidity provided by a constanly-moistened sphagnum moss support. Misting is very useful, particularly on very hot summer days, or in winter when the heating is turned up high. On such occasions, the plants, especially those with broad leaves from the tropical rain forests, will be losing large amounts of water. However, only use this method as a boost, for it will merely give temporary relief, unless carried out almost continually.

INCREASING HUMIDITY

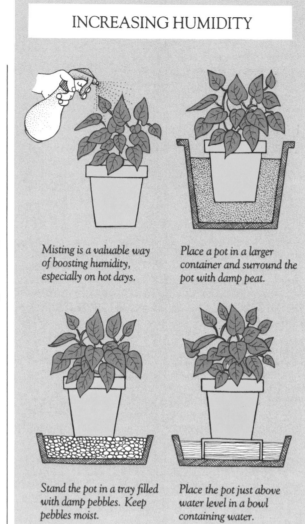

Misting is a valuable way of boosting humidity, especially on hot days.

Place a pot in a larger container and surround the pot with damp peat.

Stand the pot in a tray filled with damp pebbles. Keep pebbles moist.

Place the pot just above water level in a bowl containing water.

Humidity guide
■ Avoid waterlogging; never allow the pots to sit in water.
■ Easily-damaged leaves and flowers should not be misted.
■ Only mist during the day and early evening.
■ Increase humidity as the temperature rises.
■ Whenever possible, mist with soft, warm water. This will avoid watermarks on the foliage.
■ Keep humidifiers topped-up; peat and pebbles moistened.

COMPOST
Potting compost for house plants should be free-draining and free of all pests and diseases. For these reasons, it is essential to use a special formula, sterile mixture, with its balanced supply of nutrients, rather than to rely on the inconsistencies of garden soil.

A loam-based, John Innes compost can be made up, if sufficiently large quantities are required, but it is normally more convenient to buy it ready-mixed. This formulation is available in different strengths – 1, 2 and 3. The type required will depend on the rate of growth, or maturity, of a particular plant. Peat-based, or soil-less composts, have become increasingly popular with growers, largely because they are more competitively priced, but peat is also the ideal medium for plastic pots

on capillary watering systems. Although some plants have a particular preference (see plant directory), normally either is suitable for the majority of plants.

Compost guide
■ Soak peat-based composts thoroughly before potting-up.
■ Pot-on in the same compost to avoid having to adjust watering.
■ Loam-based composts retain less water.
■ Peat-based composts have a tendency to dry out suddenly. If this happens, completely immerse the pot in a bucket of water and leave it until the bubbles have stopped rising. First, weight the compost down to prevent it from rising out of the pot.
■ Loam-based composts in clay pots provide a more stable base for tall, top-heavy plants.

WATERING
Every plant has a varying need for water to enforce its own growth pattern. Temperature, and the relative presence of light and humidity, will also have an influence on the quantity and timing of watering.

Basic rules
■ Always examine the compost before watering. Dry surfaces do not necessarily indicate that re-watering is necessary; the compost is freqently still moist underneath. Test plastic pots by plunging a stick into the compost. It will come out either wet, or sticky, if the compost is moist. Tap the sides of clay pots; if they ring the compost is dry.
■ Ensure that a plant's cultural needs are met (see plant directory).
■ The majority of plants will not survive in a waterlogged compost as there will be insufficient air for healthy

root development. Always empty any water still remaining in saucers, or decorative containers, half an hour after watering.

The most usual method of watering is through the surface compost, but plants with corms, or dense and easily damaged foliage, are better watered from below. Stand the pots in water, so that the water is level with the top of the compost. Leave the plant to soak until the surface of the compost glistens. Remove the pot from the water, but allow it to drain thoroughly before returning it to its normal position. Always give these plants an occasional careful top watering to flush through fertilizer salts which will have risen to the surface.

Thorough watering is essential, whichever method you use; cautious dribbles never reach all the roots. It is generally better to water during the early part of the day, so that the water can be utilized by the plant during the daylight hours. Ideally, you should give soft water;

chlorine and lime deposits tend to build up on the surface of the compost, forming hard, white crusts. However, never use water softened by a home appliance because it will introduce chemicals that are unsuited to plants. If rainwater is not available, you can use hard tap water, which has been left to stand overnight.

How much water?
This will depend on the individual plant, but generally the rate of watering will be affected by:
■ The growing and flowering periods – increase water at these times. After flowering there is normally a pause before growth re-starts when less water will be needed.
■ Hot weather – check thirsty plants daily.
■ When the plant was re-potted. The more roots there are the greater the demand for water.
■ The type of pot and compost. Clay pots are highly porous and will not retain water as well as plastic pots. Loam absorbs less than peat.
■ The weather. On

sunny days plants on a windowsill will need more water than plants in shady positions.

FEEDING
A plant pot, or container, holds only limited supplies of the additional nutrients which all pot-grown plants need; these will normally be exhausted roughly two months after re-potting. The essential fertilizers are nitrogen (N), phosphorus (P) and potash (K) which promote strong leaf and root development and good flowering. The carefully balanced compound house plant fertilizers are the most convenient way of providing these elements. The best forms are the liquid, soluble powder and foliar feeds, which allow you direct control over how much and when to administer; dry tablets and sticks work on a slow-release basis which is very useful for holiday feeding, but less accurate over longer periods of time, since they cannot be stopped readily at the end of the growing season.

The fertilizers vary in chemical content, which is always shown on the packet as a ratio of N:P:K. A good general fertilizer has a high proportion of nitrogen; however a plant which is producing foliage at the expense of flowers should be given a higher proportion of potash. Lime-hating plants need a fertilizer with ammonium sulphate, which leaves an acid residue in the soil. They may also need an occasional feed with sequestrated iron to prevent yellowing growth.

Foliar feeds are useful for providing rapid tonics when routine feeding has been neglected, and for plants growing on bark. Dilution instructions are given on the packet. Remember that overfeeding can be harmful.

Never feed:
■ A sick, wilting or dormant plant.
■ A plant with dried-out compost.
■ A plant that has just been re-potted, or a healthy plant whose roots are not filling the pot.

METHODS OF FEEDING PLANTS

Spraying liquid fertilizer on to leaves is the most convenient way of feeding indoor plants.

Fertilizer mixed into the top layer of potting mixture lasts longer, but is slow to act.

Dry tablets and sticks work on a slow-release basis and are ideal for holiday feeding.

Special foliar feeds have an immediate tonic effect. Also, they are ideal for epiphytes.

POTTING

The frequency of potting-on – placing the plant in a larger-sized pot – as opposed to re-potting, or top-dressing – changing all or part of the compost – will depend on the maturity of the plant and on how quickly it is growing. Most young plants grow fast and the root ball should be inspected annually to determine whether the roots are filling the pot. Healthy, happy-growing roots will have a moist sheen and strong tips; potting-on will only be necessary if black-tipped roots are thickly filling the compost. The pot should be only one size larger.

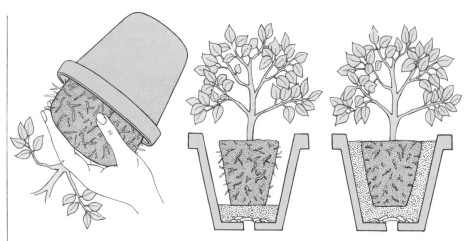

Remove the plant by supporting it with one hand and then firmly tapping the pot base.

Place drainage crocks in clay pots. Add a layer of compost. Position the root ball.

Fill the sides with moistened compost and firm down gently. Water plant thoroughly.

PRUNING

Pinching-out the growing tips of drawn, or etiolated, plants will always encourage new side shoots to grow and generally promote a bushier appearance. However, many plants also need to be occasionally pruned to control their shape. Always trim back plants when they are growing actively. When possible, trim just above a leaf which has a bud pointing in the direction you want the stem to grow in. Only remove the growing tips of specimen plants when they have reached the desired height.

Use sharp secateurs so that the stem is not bruised or crushed.

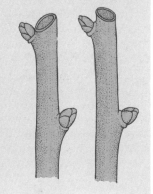

Pruning techniques ▷
Always cut stems just above a bud, sloping the cut downwards away from the bud. Incorrect (left), correct (right).

CLEANING

Regular cleaning of plants is not just a cosmetic task, for it prevents any build-up of light-reducing dust and effectively dislodges insects, eggs and mites. Clean smooth-leaved plants with a soft, moist sponge. Portable plants can be given the occasional warm shower, but always use a fine dry brush on velvety leaves. Replace plants on sunny windowsills only when the foliage is dry.

STAKING AND TRAINING

Train plants when the stems are young and most flexible, loose ties might sometimes be necessary to hold the stems in position. Place stakes in position at re-potting time when it is easier to avoid damaging the roots, but always ensure that the plant remains the main attraction.

Regular sponging of leaves will remove dust, insects, eggs and mites.

Trellis in a pot ▷
Insert support when re-potting and train the stems upwards.

TOOLS AND EQUIPMENT

Only a limited number of tools and materials are essential for house plant care, but others, such as soil moisture gauges, maximum and minimum thermometers, hygrometers (for checking humidity levels) and light meters are very useful for giving accurate indications of prevailing conditions and for allowing you to control them. Always have at least two misters, keeping one clearly marked for insecticides and fungicides. Ensure that the spray is fully adjustable and is sufficiently strong to reach all your plants. If you have limited time and large numbers of plants you might find it handy to keep several, ready-filled misters in different parts of the house. You can also set aside a bucket or bowl so that hard water can be allowed to stand, thus ensuring that supplies of suitable water are always ready. A jug is more convenient, but you should allow the water to stand for a longer period.

Thermometers
A maximum-minimum thermometer is essential if you want to measure temperature fluctuations. The results will enable you to judge whether a particular spot suits a particular plant.

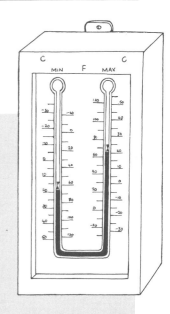

1 Moss-stick; 2 compost; 3 clay pots; 4 clay half-pots; 5 seed pan; 6 canes; 7 hygrometer; 8 soil gauge (moisture meter); 9 misters; 10 maximum-minimum thermometer; 11 trellis; 12 watering-can; 13 secateurs; 14 liquid fertilizer; 15 sponges; 16 twine; 17 spoon and fork; 18 string; 19 stakes; 20 ties.

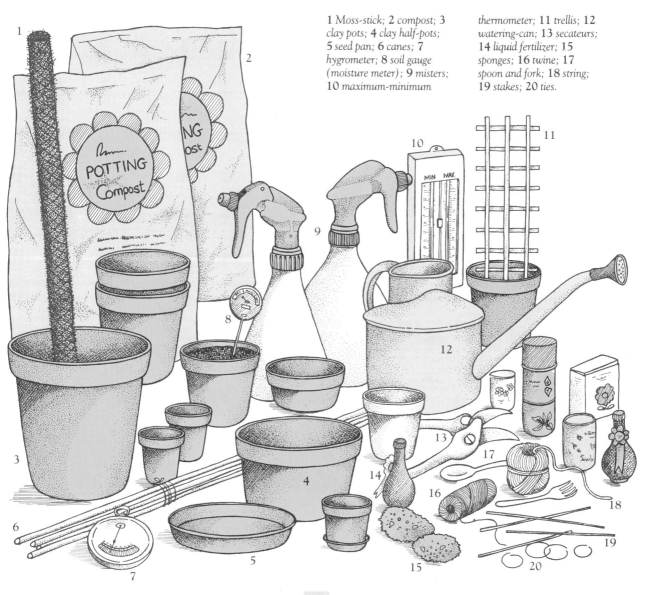

►HYDROCULTURE◄

Hydroculture, or hydroponics as it is frequently termed, is a fascinating method of growing
healthy, vigorous plants without soil, which was first discovered over 300 years ago by an
English botanist, John Wood. It was while experimenting to find out how plants received
their nutrients from the soil, that Wood established that the material itself was
unimportant and that any medium, which held sufficient air, water and nutrient and
provided firm support for the plant, was just as suitable. The refinements and advances
in this basic technique have been considerable, and today a whole industry has evolved
around it, growing large numbers of vegetables ranging from watercress to tomatoes.

HOUSE PLANT growers have
been quick to realize that
hydroculture stimulates
rapid, lush growth and
minimizes maintenance by
controlling the problems
associated with watering and
by obliterating soil-borne
pests and diseases. The
higher levels of humidity
discourage red spider mite
and solve the problems
associated with dry air.
Large-scale interior planting
schemes are frequently grown
in hydroculture, and,
although it is a more
expensive method of growing
plants within the home, the
advantages the system has to
offer make it a tempting
proposition, especially when
your time is limited.

**The principle of
hydroculture**
The system uses special ion-
exchange fertilizers, which
absorb all the impurities in
the water while giving out
nutrients and essential trace
elements. The fertilizer is
attached to tiny polystyrene
granules, which means that
the process can be reversed
— in other words, that when
the water level drops, the
granules will re-absorb the
nutrients and give out the
calcium, fluoride and
chloride, thus restoring the
balance. The nutrient supply
will also cut off completely
when equilibrium is reached.
The fertilizer is always mixed
with the water, and together

they form what is known as
the nutrient solution, which
is placed in an outer
container.

An inner container, or
growing pot, contains the
soil-free roots of the plant,
which are held firmly in
position by porous clay
granules, known as leca
(Lightweight Expanded
Clay Aggregate). Ideally,
these irregularly-shaped
"pebbles" should be just
under 25 mm (1in) in
diameter. Their honeycomb
centres, surrounded by a
dense outer layer, combine
excellent water holding
ability, with firm anchorage
for the roots and set up a
capillary action which keeps
all the pebbles moist.

Plants are always placed in
separate growing pots and
then positioned singly, or
in groups, in the outer
container. This means that it
is a simple procedure to re-
arrange, or remove, plants.
Growing pots are always
quite large because they
must hold sufficient leca to
stabilize the pot. Root space
is never a problem since the
roots will happily develop
through the slits in the sides
of the pot, which also ensure
a sufficient supply of air.
Good root aeration is as
important for plants grown
in hydroculture as it is for
those grown in soil, so,
although these slots provide
some of the air, a good
airflow is also assured by the

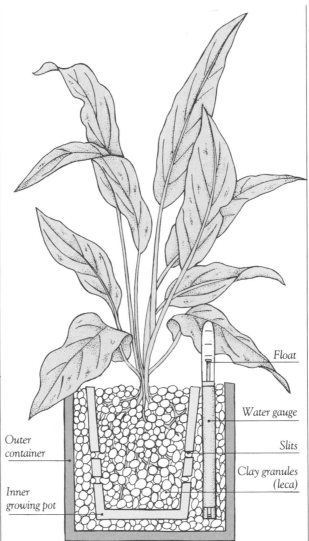

Pot plant hydroculture
*The roots of the plant should
always be soil-free and the inner
pot should have slits to allow for
root aeration. The water gauge*

*rises and falls with the water
level. When the container is one
third full, the gauge will indicate
that the maximum level has
been reached.*

Float

Water gauge

Slits

Clay granules
(leca)

Outer
container

Inner
growing pot

PLANTING IN HYDROCULTURE

Follow these simple step-by-step instructions for planting in hydroculture.

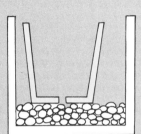
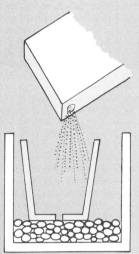

Line the base of the outer container with pre-washed, soaked leca.

Add the ion-exchange fertilizer. Quantities will be on package.

Position growing pot so that its top is just below the rim of the outer pot.

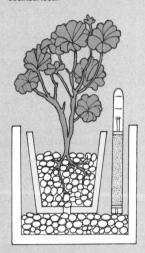
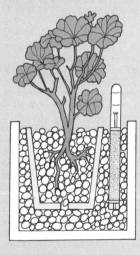
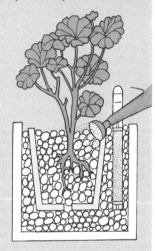

Place water gauge between the outer and inner containers.

Fill the outer container with leca until the rim of growing pot is hidden.

Add water until the gauge shows maximum, then allow container to dry out.

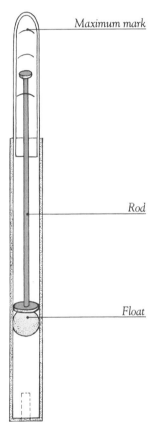

Maximum mark

Rod

Float

Water gauge
Cross-section of a water gauge used to indicate the water level in a hydroculture unit.

gap between the outer and inner containers.

This gap also provides space for the water gauge, an essential piece of equipment that measures the amount of water in the container accurately. The device consists of a float attached to a rod, which is just long enough not to be seen above the leca in the absence of water. The float rests on the water's surface, rising and falling with the level. A "maximum" mark shows when the container is one third full — this really is the maximum, as otherwise the supplies of oxygen will be insufficient to support all the plants.

First steps
Setting up a unit is simply a matter of placing sufficient quantities of pre-washed, and thoroughly soaked, leca in the base of the outer container, so that the top of the growing pot will rest just below its rim. Next, add the ion-exchange fertilizer; this comes either as a "battery" to be placed in a special compartment in the pot, or as loose granules which you spread over the leca. Quantities will vary, depending on the size of the pot, but will always be given on the packaging. One dose normally is sufficient for six months. The growing pot(s) may now be positioned and the water gauge firmly placed down the side. The entire surface should then be covered with leca, so that the rim of the growing pot is hidden — this discourages the development of algae,

since it ensures that no light will fall on the nutrient solution. The final stage is to add water.

On the first occasion, the water should be added until the gauge is showing "maximum", because both plant and leca initially absorb a great deal of water. However, before watering again, allow the container to dry out thoroughly. Wait until two days after the gauge shows minimum water level has been reached. This ensures that all the air pockets in the leca are thoroughly emptied and that enough air is taken into the rooting regions. The container should then be filled halfway between maximum and minimum. Only use the maximum level if you are going away for several weeks, or if you are growing particularly thirsty plants. Ideally the water level should only take four weeks to sink.

Maintenance

The hydroculture system removes the major worry from house plant maintenance, but it is still important to provide plants with correct levels of light and to provide enough warmth. Grow plants with similar demands together and clean foliage regularly to ensure sufficient light to support the almost continuous growth of some plants. Plants which are resting during the winter will take less water. Keep the level lower to ensure that it is used up every four weeks.

Root temperature is critical for plants grown in hydroculture. If the containers are sitting on a cold floor, place some polystyrene under them to protect them from the cold. When it is impossible to avoid low temperatures, keep the water level very low. Although the plants will not grow in these conditions,

they will survive until the spring.

Always give ordinary, warm tap water. The ion-exchange works because impurities are present. Add a few drops of house plant fertilizer to very soft water in order to start the reaction.

Plants should be potted-on infrequently, it is only ever necessary to provide a larger, more stable base for heavy top-growth. Carefully cut away the old pot and add more leca when planting in the new, larger pot. Frequent pruning will help to control the top growth.

Selecting suitable plants

Special soil-free plants are sold for hydroculture, and they are available in ever-increasing varieties. Members of the Araceae family, which includes philodendrons, *Scindapsus*, and *Aglaonema*, grow particularly well, but splendid displays of

Schefflera, *Dracaena* and ferns, as well as the elegant *Ficus benjamina*, will also flourish. Fortunately the growth in the market has encouraged growers to experiment beyond a "standard" range. Surprisingly, even plants with a distinct preference for dryness around their roots, such as *Sansevieria* and some cacti, grow well. The only foliage plant which is positively not recommended is *Hedera*; this is due to the high risk of attack by red spider mite.

Unfortunately, the increasingly varied selection of foliage house plants, which are available for growing in hydroculture, is not matched by flowering plants. This is probably because, until quite recently, hydroculture was used mainly for offices and other business premises, where the higher lighting levels demanded by most flowering plants are

CONVERTING A SOIL-ROOTED PLANT TO HYDROCULTURE

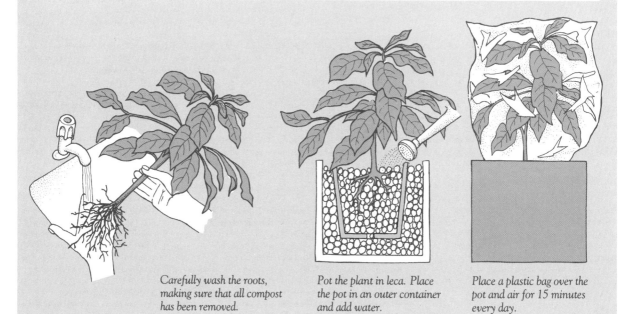

Carefully wash the roots, making sure that all compost has been removed.

Pot the plant in leca. Place the pot in an outer container and add water.

Place a plastic bag over the pot and air for 15 minutes every day.

not readily available. In addition, maintenance costs are obviously an important consideration for business users, and flowering plants rarely match the low care demands of the foliage groups. However, as an increasingly large number of people become fascinated by this exciting system, growers may start to extend their range of plants.

For those who want to include flowering plants in their displays, it is possible to cheat slightly and to include the occasional flowering house plant still growing in its soil. Make a place in the inner container with an empty flowerpot, partially filled with leca; the potted plant will grow happily inside this space, where it will be able to absorb water from below. It can be readily replaced when the flowers fade. There are two flowering members of the Araceae family which grow well when placed in a bright position — *Anthurium* and *Spathiphyllum. Anthurium* however, reacts very strongly to any alkali around its roots and should never be grown with *Dieffenbachia, Aglaonema, Peperomia* and Piper or African violets, since their discarded roots will increase the alkalinity in the nutrient solutions. Instead, grow it with the *Philodendron* or *Ficus* species or with *Schefflera, Syngonium, Cissus* and *Scindapsus.*

Plants which you want to grow, but which are difficult to obtain, may be converted to hydroculture. It is a tedious task, but worth the effort for the serious indoor gardener. It is always best to use young, growing plants, as these are more able to withstand the shock of conversion. The roots must be thoroughly, but very

carefully, washed so that every speck of compost is removed. Pot the plant in leca, ensuring that the roots sit only in the upper two-thirds of the pot. It is most important that they do not sit in water, so try to distribute them evenly. Place the pot in an outer container and add water, but not the nutrient. Then place a plastic bag over the plant to reduce the evaporation. Air the plant for about 15 minutes every day when the bag fills up with condensation. Fresh root formation is indicated when the leaves become straighter and firmer. The nutrient may now be added.

A simpler alternative is to root cuttings taken from pruned plants. Many leaf and stem cuttings may readily be rooted in leca and water. Add a little nutrient when they are strongly growing and pot-on, using the method described above.

Automatic watering systems
An alternative to growing plants in hydroculture is to use an automatic watering system. There are several types available for the home. If you have sufficient space, the system can be set up on a permanent basis. Otherwise, particularly if you are away frequently, it might be worth considering acquiring one for temporary use.

The various types of system work on the same basic principle. Purpose-built trays, which hold sand or capillary matting, are kept permanently moist by an automatic dispenser, which is attached to the main water supply. The pots must be firmly pressed into the trays, so that water may be drawn up through the drainage holes. Plastic pots are ideal for this, but the clay type will work as long as the

Self-watering in the conservatory
Line bench with polythene, cover it with sand and stand the pots on it. An automatic watering device keeps the sand permanently moist.

crocks are removed and a wick, or bandage, is placed in their base.

An alternative solution is the use of self-watering containers. These have a reservoir under their base, which is filled through a shaft running down one side, and some may also have a gauge which indicates the water level. They automatically maintain the correct level of moisture in the soil, and because they only need to be re-filled three or four times a year, frequently make very useful permanent additions. However, because water is taken up at the rate demanded by the thirstiest

plant it is essential that only plants with similar demands are grown together.

Other methods of self-watering are ideal for short holiday periods (*see p 153*), but the supply of water does not vary so it is unwise to rely on them for longer than two to three weeks. A wick may be pushed into the top of the compost and its other end placed in a tray of water; or you can use an automatic diffuser that will slowly feed water into the compost.

Another solution is to place as many plants as possible into a bath lined with capillary matting, remove the plug and leave a tap slowly dripping.

SELF-HELP GUIDE

THE BEST WAY to avoid pests and diseases is to keep the compost surrounding the plant scrupulously clean, and to control humidity. Regular and thorough checking of all plants will ensure that any threatened plant is isolated rapidly before the pests or diseases are transmitted to the rest of your collection. The most common causes of plant failure are cultural. An inspection of the compost will often provide the answer. Watering problems are the most obvious cause, but the plants may need re-potting, or the roots may be under attack, particularly if the pot was not cleaned before potting. Less obvious problems will normally be solved by a quick check through the plant directory and the general care section.

The important thing is not to ignore the plant with the vague hope that it will cure itself. Also, do not panic and kill the plant by an excess of kindness. If it is beyond help, establish why, and then throw it out quickly – there is nothing so depressing as a dying plant.

CULTURAL PROBLEMS

Overwatering	Lower leaves – limp, soft, rotting or turning yellow. Soft, darkening stems. Soggy soil. Flower drop. Green slime on compost surface and on the sides of clay pots.
Underwatering	Leaves and stem wilting. Leaf edges dry and curling under. Brown leaf tips. Mature leaves drop. Fast-fading flowers. **Dry sphagnum moss stick or aerial roots not bedded in.** New leaves do not develop. Upper leaves and stem wilt. and stem.
Dry air	Leaf edges – brown. Leaf drop.
Overheating	Lower leaves dry up and drop. Flowers fade fast. Spindly growth in a good winter light.
Rapid changes	Sudden yellowing and dropping of leaves.
Poor light	Etiolated stems stretching towards source of light. New leaves – pale and small. No flowerbuds. Plain leaves on variegated plants.
Intense light	Crisp, brown leaves on one side. Pale foliage. Leaves with yellow, or brown, spots and patches.
Overfeeding	New growth rapid, but weak. General wilting. White crust on surface of compost. **Too much nitrogen** Very vigorous growth, healthy foliage, poor flowering. **Lime in the compost of acid-loving plants** Lanky growth. Yellow leaves which do not drop.
Underfeeding	Poor growth. Leaves fade to pale green; lower leaves yellowing and dropping. Small new leaves.
The abused plant	White, or yellow, spotting on healthy foliage. Balding of hairy and downy foliage – careless watering. Brown tips when grown in good cultural conditions – knocking by pets or humans.
Re-potting required	Rapid wilting. Poor growth. Roots sprouting through surface, and drainage holes. Plant rising from pot.

DISEASES

Name	Cause	Symptom	Control
Botrytis cinerea (grey mould)	High humidity with no ventilation – normally occurs in winter.	Grey-brown furry mould, covering stems, leaves and flowerbuds.	Destroy infected plant. Fumigate conservatory with fungicidal spray. Avoid overwatering, overfeeding and overcrowded conditions. Keep water off delicate leaves.
Virus	Usually transmitted by insects.	Leaves blotched or mottled with yellow. Flowers develop large white streaks. Stunted distorted growth.	Destroy infected plant.
Black-leg	Overwatering, or compacted soil.	Rotting at base of stems.	Destroy plant.
Mildew	Overwatering and inadequate ventilation.	White, powdery coating, on stems, leaves and possibly flowers.	Cut away infected part of plant and treat with benomyl.
Rust	Dank, airless conditions.	Powdery, red-brown, spots and patches on the underside of leaves.	Remove infected parts, spray with mancozeb.
Sooty mould	Grows on honeydew deposits, left by scale, mealy bug, aphids and whitefly.	Black fungus and eventual stunted growth.	Wipe off with damp cloth. Ensure pests do not attack again.
Oedema, or corky scab	Lack of light, waterlogging.	Hard, corky growths on the undersides of leaves.	Destroy badly affected plants. Improve cultural conditions of survivors.
Root rot	Fungal decay, due to waterlogging.	Yellowing and wilting of leaves rapidly followed by plant failure.	May be possible to sever affected roots. Water less in future, check compost.
Leaf spot	Fungal or bacterial decay, due to damp conditions.	Small brown spots rapidly enlarge to cover entire leaf.	Remove damaged parts and spray with benomyl. Do not mist for several weeks.
Basal rot	Overwatering, lack of ventilation and heat.	General wilting.	Try to cut infected area away or destroy plant.

PESTS

Pest	Damage	Control
Aphids common plant lice which may be green, black-red or white. About 3mm (⅛in) long.	Suck out the plant's juices, stunt new growth, foliage pales, curls back and dies. Secrete sticky honeydew, that frequently attracts sooty black mould. Attack soft young tips, or the underside of leaves.	Pick off and crush any visible aphids, then wash plant, either by dunking in warm soapy water, or swab with a soft soapy cloth. Spray seriously infested plants with malathion – in a well-ventilated area, or outside. Rinse leaves when dry.
White flies adults are very tiny and flutter off plants when disturbed. Eggs laid on the underside of leaves and hatch into almost invisible green larvae – these inflict the most damage.	Leaves turn yellow and drop. May eventually kill plant. Secrete honeydew.	Wash the leaves with a strong spray of tepid water. Alternatively, treat serious attacks with malathion – either outside, or in a well-ventilated area. Rinse leaves when dry.
Red spider mite either orange-red or yellow-green. Very difficult to see with the naked eye.	Suck the sap, resulting in finely mottled, pale-green foliage. Usually found, spinning their webs, on the underside of leaves. Plants become stunted and die.	Dislodge with strong spray of tepid water, or wipe with a soft, soapy cloth and then rinse. Alternatively, spray with malathion (as above). If the mites persist, destroy the plant.
Scales hard outer shells, coloured yellowish-greenish-brown. Young very mobile; adults do not move.	May encrust stems and leaves like bumpy blisters, cause stunted, skeletal plants, yellow leaves and possible failure of plant. Leave honeydew deposits.	Gently scrub off young, using warm soapy water, or spray with malathion. Rinse well. Swab adults with methylated spirits, allow to dry before dislodging.
Mealy bugs soft 6mm (¼in) bodies covered with white powdery wax – look like blobs of cotton wool.	General yellowing, deformity and stunted growth. Eventually kill plants.	Swab with methylated spirits, wash the plant thoroughly when clear of infestation. Spray severely attacked plants with malathion.
Cyclamen mite minuscule mites which are very difficult to spot.	Curling of outer leaves, rotting or withering of stems, flowers, and flowerbuds.	No effective control, remove damaged foliage instantly to avoid total plant failure.
Thrips tiny, black-winged insects. Readily spotted when plants are shaken over a piece of white paper.	Suck the plant tissues, causing white mottling, often surrounded by small black specks.	Shake off and destroy with lukewarm water, or spray with malathion.
Worms	Slow draining compost, caused by casts, or by the worms themselves.	Examine compost and remove worms – return them to the garden. Clear drainage holes before re-potting.

Note malathion is not suitable for use on ferns, petunias or pileas. Instead, use derris powder to treat infestation on these plants.

HOLIDAY CARE

The time when you take your holiday, or go away for a long weekend, will be the most traumatic for your plants, unless you make some provision for their care. The best solution is to ask another sympathetic plant grower to come in regularly to look after them. It is a wise precaution to show them where every plant is and to explain individual requirements.

Always remove plants from windowsills in case of unexpected heatwaves or frosts.

Group plants together in appropriate places, which should, of course, still reflect their cultural requirements. This will facilitate watering, as well as ensuring that a lone plant will not be forgotten.

Place a slow-release fertilizer stick, or tablet, in the compost of plants which would normally be fed during this period.

If you have central heating and you go away in winter, leave it on a very low heat to ensure that the plants' minimum temperature requirements are met.

If you plants are grown in hydroculture (see pp 146-9), ensure that the unit is filled to maximum before you leave. If you are away for longer than five weeks, you should arrange to have the unit topped up again.

Automatic watering systems (see pp 146-9) will have to be set up correctly. Choose the system most suited to the length of time you will be away.

During the summer, any reduction in the amount of water lost through transpiration will ease the demand for water. This reduction will certainly be assisted by the removal of plants from bright positions.

In addition, small plants can be enclosed in polythene bags, which will return the transpired water to the compost.

First, water the plant thoroughly, and then place it in a large bag. One end of the bag should be tied loosely around the stem, so that there is just enough space for the drips to trickle down on to the compost. Tie the other end of the bag over the top of the plant, leaving a small opening for air to enter. This method will normally keep a plant fresh for three weeks.

If you are away for a long period in summer, it is important that plants receive copious supplies of water or they will not survive.

During the summer, many plants will benefit from a spell outside in a suitable shady position, if you can arrange for this to be done.

When you return, carefully check every plant. If necessary, give them a thorough drink and feed before returning them to their usual places.

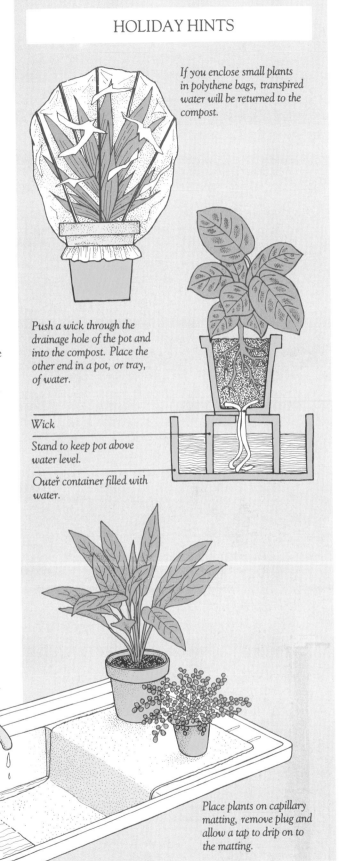

HOLIDAY HINTS

If you enclose small plants in polythene bags, transpired water will be returned to the compost.

Push a wick through the drainage hole of the pot and into the compost. Place the other end in a pot, or tray, of water.

Wick

Stand to keep pot above water level.

Outer container filled with water.

Place plants on capillary matting, remove plug and allow a tap to drip on to the matting.

INDEX

ACKNOWLEDGEMENTS

The Paul Press Ltd and the authors would like to thank the following persons and organizations, to whom copyright in the photographs noted belongs:

7 Michael Boys; 8 Michael Boys; 10 EWA Photo Library/Michael Dunne; 11 Camera Press; 12/13 EWA/Geoffrey Frosh; 14 Michael Boys; 15 Tania Midgley; 16 EWA/Michael Nicholson; 17 EWA/Neil Lorimer; 18 Camera Press; 19 EWA/Michael Dunne; 20 EWA/Clive Helme; 21/23 Michael Boys/Susan Griggs Agency; 24 Michael Boys; 25 EWA/Michael Nicholson; 26/27 David Brittain/Good Housekeeping magazine; 29 EWA/Michael Dunne; 30 Camera Press; 31 EWA/Neil Lorimer; 32/33 Michael Boys; 34/35/36/37 Camera Press; 39/40 Tania Midgley; 41 Michael Boys; 42 The Design Council; 43 EWA/Michael Nicholson; 45 Jon Bouchier; 46 Jessica Strang; 47 Camera Press; 48/49 Jon Bouchier; 50 Camera Press; 51 Harry Smith Collection; 53 Camera Press; 55 Camera Press; 56 Photos Horticultural; 58 Bernard Alfieri; 59 Photos Horticultural; 60 EWA/Michael Nicholson; 61 EWA/David Lloyd; 63 Camera Press; 64 Hans Reinhard/Bruce Coleman Ltd; 65/66 Photos Horticultural; 67 Eric Crichton/ Bruce Coleman Ltd; 68 Bernard Alfieri; 69 Eric Crichton/Bruce Coleman Ltd; 70/71 Photos Horticultural; 72 Adrian Davies/Bruce Coleman Ltd; 73 Photos Horticultural; 74 Michael Boys; 76/77 Michael Boys; 77 EWA/Neil Lorimer; 78 EWA/Gary Chowawitz; 81 Antony Johnson; 82 John Knights; 84 EWA/Rodney Hyett; 85 Camera Press; 86 EWA/Michael Dunne; 87 Terence Soames/Rochford Landscape Ltd; 88/89 Michael Boys; 90/91 Terence Soames/Rochford Landscape Ltd

Front cover Michael Boys
Back cover Camera Press; Jon Bouchier

The authors and publisher would also like to thank: David Welch, Director, Leisure and Recreation Department, City of Aberdeen for his assistance in identifying the cacti and succulents on pp 55 & 56. and First Front Garage, Kennington for permission to photograph their premises.